ultimate

weird but true!

3

With water surging over the rocks nearby, ice climber Will Gadd scrambles up a frozen area of Niagara Falls, New York, U.S.A., scaling a 147-foot (45-m)-high wall of jagged ice.

NATIONAL
GEOGRAPHIC
KiDS

ultimate
weird
but
true!

3

NATIONAL GEOGRAPHIC

WASHINGTON, D.C.

contents

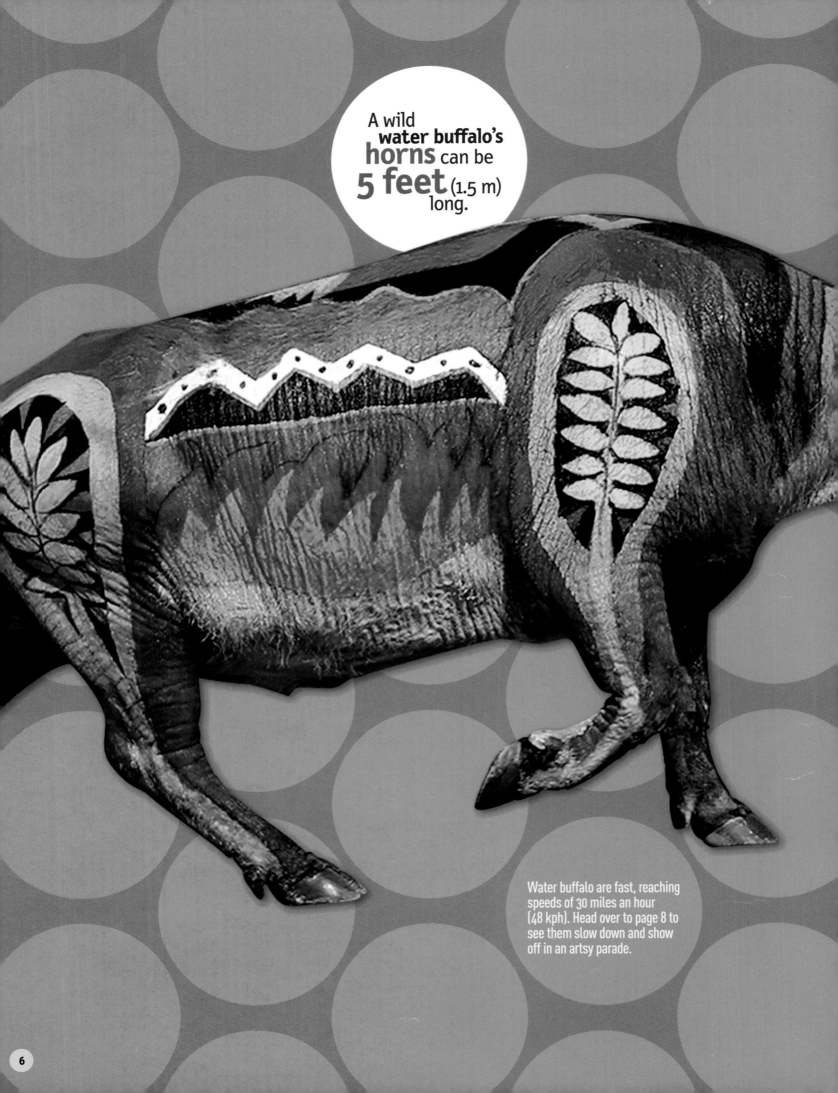

A wild **water buffalo's** **horns** can be **5 feet** (1.5 m) long.

Water buffalo are fast, reaching speeds of 30 miles an hour (48 kph). Head over to page 8 to see them slow down and show off in an artsy parade.

CHAPTER 1

ULTiMaTE EXTReMES

Weird
CONTESTS

CONTESTANTS COMPETE TO **EAT** THE MOST OF THESE TONGUE-TINGLING LEAVES AT ENGLAND'S **STINGING NETTLE** COMPETITION. **OUCH!**

>>> FROM **MANLY MUSTACHES** TO **MUTTONCHOPS,** PRIZES ARE AWARDED FOR **EXTREME FACIAL HAIR** AT THE **WORLD BEARD** AND **MUSTACHE CHAMPIONSHIP!**

SOME 50 **WILDLY PAINTED WATER BUFFALO** >>> STRUT THEIR STUFF AT THIS ANNUAL COMPETITION IN CHINA. THE MOST **BEAUTIFUL BEAST** WINS.

<<< EVER SINCE 1267, THE PERSON PULLING THE **GOOFIEST FACE** WHILE WEARING A **HORSE COLLAR** HAS WON TOP PRIZE AT ENGLAND'S **WORLD GURNING COMPETITION.**

>>>

AT THE **WIFE CARRYING** WORLD CHAMPIONSHIPS, IN FINLAND, BURLY TYPES MUST RUN AN **832-FOOT** (254-M) **TRACK** IN 60 SECONDS.

MUD >>> **LOVERS** SWIM A **60-YARD** (55-M) TRENCH AT THE ANNUAL **BOG SNORKELING** CHAMPIONSHIP IN WALES!

In just FIVE SECONDS an

AVALANCHE

can reach SPEEDS up to
200 miles an hour (130 kph).
That's as fast as a RACE CAR!

A mass of SLIDING SNOW can weigh as much as ONE MILLION TONS
(907,000 t).

ultimate secret revealed!

How does an avalanche hit such superfast speeds? Of the two types of avalanches—slab and loose snow—slab is the fastest. It often occurs after heavy snowfall, when layers beneath new snow can no longer support the additional weight. Suddenly, the packed snow on top breaks away and starts to move as a single slab, picking up more snow as it goes. Anything traveling downhill gathers speed, but add heavy snow to strong winds and steep mountain slopes, and WHOOSH!

A PYGMY SHREW

THAT'S AS IF **YOU** FEASTED ON . . .

4 watermelons

or 10 gallons of milk

EATS **1.3** TIMES
ITS BODY WEIGHT
EVERY DAY—

or 30 birthday cakes

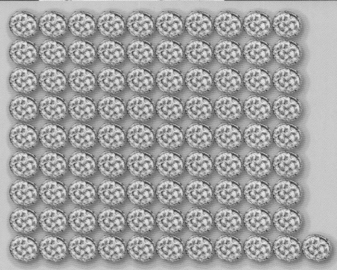

or 91 pizzas

<<< Rainbow Rock

WHAT IS IT?
Fly Geyser, Nevada, U.S.A.

WHY IT'S AWESOME:
The **water** gushing from these springs is **boiling hot.** Heat-loving **algae** create rainbow colors on the rocks.

Absolutely
AWESOME
Places

>>> Sci-fi Mountain

WHAT IS IT?
Avatar Hallelujah Mountain, China

WHY IT'S AWESOME:
As if floating in air, this 3,540-foot (1,080-m) **rock tower** inspired the levitating islands in the blockbuster movie *Avatar.*

No Surfing Allowed

WHAT IS IT?
Wave Rock, Hyden, Australia

WHY IT'S AWESOME:
Formed 2.7 billion years ago, this ancient 49-foot (15-m)-high **granite** rock **predates dinosaurs.**

WHAT IS IT?
Spotted Lake, British Columbia, Canada

WHY IT'S AWESOME:
The spots come out in the summer, when most of the lake water **evaporates** to reveal colorful pools of **mineral deposits.**

Polka-dot Lake

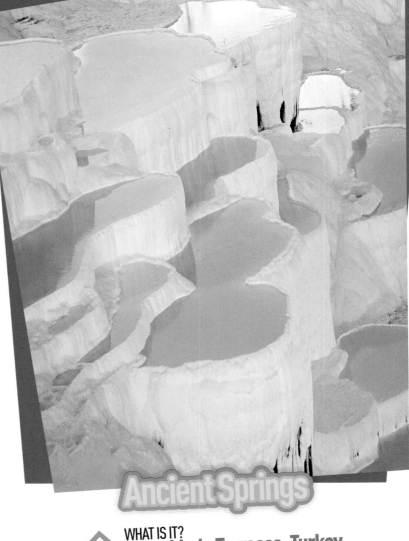

Ancient Springs

Fire Pit

WHAT IS IT?
Darvaza Crater, Turkmenistan

WHY IT'S AWESOME:
This **crater** appeared in a natural gas field 40 years ago. Lit to burn off **poisonous** gases, it has been **burning** ever since.

WHAT IS IT?
Pamukkale Terraces, Turkey

WHY IT'S AWESOME:
Minerals deposited by hot **spring water** have hardened to create dazzling, white terraces. The ancient Greeks liked to **bathe** here.

on target

CHECK OUT THESE COOL FACTS ABOUT THIS **SHARPSHOOTING FISH.** WHO KNEW FISH HAD SUCH **GREAT AIM?**

ARCHERFISH catch prey by firing **WATER JETS** up to **6.5 FEET** (2 m) into the **AIR.**

The fish **ADJUST** their **SHOOTING ANGLE** for **PINPOINT ACCURACY.**

The fish **RAPIDLY FIRE**, aiming up to **7 POWERFUL SQUIRTS** in quick **SUCCESSION.**

The **FORCE** of the **WATER JETS** makes **INSECTS** and even **SMALL LIZARDS TOPPLE** from **LEAVES** and **BRANCHES.**

If **PREY** is **CLOSE** enough, archerfish can **JUMP 12 INCHES** (30 cm) **OUT** of the **WATER** and **SNATCH** it in their **MOUTHS.**

ARCHERFISH live in GROUPS and LEARN how to SHOOT from EACH OTHER.

BLACK and WHITE STRIPES provide CAMOUFLAGE UNDER the water.

Archerfish GROW up to 6 INCHES (15 cm) long and live in RIVERS and STREAMS in ASIA.

The fish manipulates its TONGUE and SQUEEZES its GILLS to propel WATER through its MOUTH.

Archerfish CONTROL the SPEED of their water jets by CHANGING the way they OPEN and CLOSE their MOUTHS.

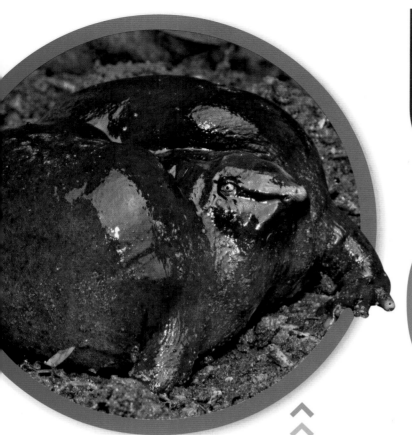

UGLY
BUT *TOTALLY*
COOL
ANIMALS

THERE'S MORE TO THE **PIG-NOSED FROG** THAN ITS **ODD SNOUT.** THIS INDIAN **AMPHIBIAN** ALSO **CLUCKS** LIKE A CHICKEN.

WITH **EYES** ON THE TOP OF ITS HEAD, THE **STARGAZER** EASILY SPIES **PREY** SWIMMING OVERHEAD.

<<< **ALIEN LANDING!** THE **PRICKLY GLOBES** OF THIS **TREEHOPPER** ARE **FREAKY** ENOUGH TO KEEP SPIDERS AND BIRDS AWAY.

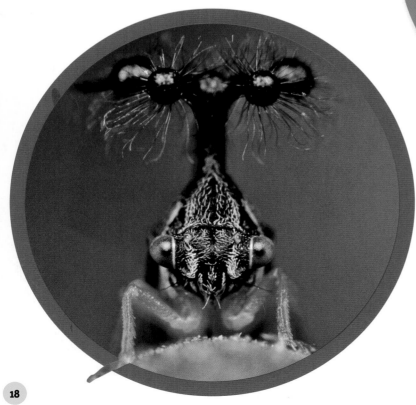

PASSING **FISH** THINK THE MATAMATA TURTLE IS JUST A PILE OF **OLD BROWN LEAVES** ∨∨∨ UNTIL THEY'RE **SNAPPED UP** FOR DINNER.

∧∧∧ THE **CHINESE CRESTED DOG** HAS HAIR ONLY ON ITS **HEAD, TAIL,** AND **FEET.** THE ANCIENT CHINESE BELIEVED IT HAD **HEALING POWERS.**

<<< A **KING VULTURE'S** COLORFUL **BEAK** IS THICK AND STRONG—THE PERFECT TOOL FOR SHREDDING THE **DEAD ANIMALS** IT EATS!

THRILL-SEEKERS

balance barefoot on **sky-high slacklines** in the Italian Alps.

→ Each year **500 extreme athletes** gather at Monte Piana, Italy, for the International Highline Meeting.

→ Athletes gather not to compete, but to practice and learn from one another.

→ The **lines** are suspended **7,625 feet** (2,324 m) above the **gorge**.

→ The slacklines are not pulled tight across the gorge. They lack **tension**—hence their name—to allow more **bounce** and **movement** from side to side.

→ Participants **rest** in **hammocks** that hang from the slacklines. Some even **sleep there!**

8 CRAZY

IN **CALIFORNIA,** U.S.A., IT IS ILLEGAL TO EAT AN **ORANGE** IN THE **BATHTUB.**

A **LAW** limits **MOURNERS** at **FUNERALS** in **MASSACHUSETTS,** U.S.A., to just **3 SANDWiCHES** EACH.

EATING **FRIED CHICKEN** with anything other than your fingers is **OUTLAWED** in **Gainesville, Georgia,** U.S.A.

IN **SINGAPORE,** chewing gum IS ONLY AVAILABLE WITH A PRESCRIPTION.

LAWS ABOUT FOOD

IN **MEMPHIS, TENNESSEE,** U.S.A., A LAW MAKES IT **ILLEGAL** TO TAKE **LEFTOVER PIE**

HOME FROM A **RESTAURANT.**

In **WISCONSIN,** U.S.A., it is illegal to serve **MARGARiNE** in **SCHOOLS** and **HOSPITALS.**

IN **FRANCE, KETCHUP** IS **BANNED** IN ELEMENTARY SCHOOLS.

IT'S AGAINST THE LAW IN **KENTUCKY,** U.S.A., TO CARRY AN **ICE-CREAM CONE** IN YOUR **POCKET.**

REAL-LIFE ICE MAN

MOST PEOPLE COULD NOT SURVIVE SUBZERO TEMPERATURES FOR LONGER THAN A FEW MINUTES, BUT WIM HOF DOESN'T EVEN SHIVER!

WIM HOF TRAINS HIS BODY USING YOGA, BREATHING, AND DEEP MEDITATION.

HE IS ABLE TO MAINTAIN A CORE BODY TEMPERATURE OF 98.6°F (37°C). THIS KEEPS HIM FROM FREEZING.

This **DAREDEVIL** is **cold-proof!** He has trained his BODY to endure extreme temperatures.

HOF'S ICY STUNTS RAISE MONEY FOR CHARITY AND AWARENESS ABOUT CLIMATE CHANGE.

FastFACTS

WHO: Wim Hof

WHAT: Demonstrated his ability to withstand ice-cold temperatures of 32°F (0°C) and below

HOW LONG: 1 hour and 52 minutes and 42 seconds

WHERE: New York City, U.S.A.

WHEN: November 17, 2011

Subzero STUNTS

Hof holds over 21 Guinness records.

He ran a 26-mile (42-km) marathon in temperatures as low as -4°F (-20°C) while barefoot and wearing only shorts.

He swam 217 feet (66 m) under the frozen surface of a Finnish lake with one breath, wearing just shorts and goggles.

He climbed Tanzania's Mt. Kilimanjaro (19,340 ft/5,895 m) wearing just shorts and shoes. Temperatures at the summit can reach -15°F (-26°C).

25

Without **gel** and **hair spray,** this man's **hair** reaches his **knees!**

It takes three stylists, one bottle of gel, and three cans of hair spray to make this hair stand on end. Check out other zany hair facts on page 38.

26

CHAPTER 2

LARGER than LIFE

FABULOUS FLUFF!
THIS RABBIT'S FUR IS OVER 1 FOOT (30 CM) LONG.

ENGLISH **ANGORA BUNNIES** CAN BE **WHITE, CREAM, BLACK, OR BROWN.**

AFTER A **TRIM**, THE **FUR GROWS BACK** AT ABOUT 1 **INCH** (2.5 CM) A MONTH.

LILIANNA IS THE ONLY ANGORA RABBIT TO WIN OPEN BEST IN SHOW.

BREEDER BETTY CHU HAS SHOWN HER OUT-OF-THIS-WORLD ANGORAS ON A GAME SHOW!

WHEN LILIANNA HAS A TRIM, HER FUR IS USED FOR MAKING SOCKS, HATS, AND GLOVES.

supersize
STUFF

<<< IT TAKES A **2-FOOT-LONG** (61-CM) **NAIL FILE** TO KEEP AN ELEPHANT'S **MASSIVE FEET** IN SHAPE.

>>> IN MELBOURNE, AUSTRALIA, THE **WICKED WITCH'S RUBY SLIPPERS** COME IN EXTRA LARGE! THEY'RE **11.5 FEET** LONG. (3.5 M)

<<< **700,000 RUBBER BANDS** MADE THIS **GIGANTIC BALL** IN FLORIDA, U.S.A. IT WEIGHS **9,032 POUNDS!** (4,097 KG)

700,000 FLOWERS

MAKE THE PATTERN IN THIS **COLOSSAL CARPET** IN BELGIUM.

THIS **37-FOOT-** (11-M) HIGH **SAND CASTLE** IN NEW JERSEY, U.S.A., IS AS TALL AS **TWO GIRAFFES!**

HUNGRY? IT TOOK A TEAM IN FLORIDA, U.S.A., **THREE HOURS** TO COOK THIS **125.5-POUND** (57-KG) >>> **HOT DOG!**

MEGA MOLLUSK

This oversize **KITE** weighs **6 TIMES** as much as a real octopus and is as **LONG** as a **football field.**

FastFACTS

WHAT: Monster-size "Mollusk Octopus" kite

WHERE: Hohhot First Kite Festival, Xilamuren Grassland, China

WHEN: August 2014

WHO: Heige Kite Team, Tianjin, China

SIZE: 361 feet (110 m) long by 49 feet (15 m) wide

THE CHINESE STARTED FLYING KITES MORE THAN 2,000 YEARS AGO.

EARLY CHINESE KITES WERE SHAPED LIKE DELICATE BIRDS AND MADE FROM SILK AND BAMBOO.

Up in the AIR

This giant kite was so big and heavy that it took 30 people to get it into the air. Mother Nature helped, too. They didn't work alone, either. The festival is held in one of the windiest places in China—powerful gusts sweep in from the Gobi desert, giving these huge kites that extra lift.

MOST OF THIS TENTACLED SPECTACLE IS MADE OF KITE NYLON, A LIGHTWEIGHT MATERIAL THAT STOPS WATER FROM GETTING INSIDE.

THE LARGEST REAL OCTOPUS EVER FOUND WAS 11 FEET (3.4 M) LONG. THIS HIGHFLIER IS 30 TIMES THAT!

GIANT JELLYFISH, FLOWERS, AND PANDAS ALSO TOOK TO THE SKIES AT THIS FESTIVAL.

THE FESTIVAL ATTRACTED 35 TEAMS FROM ALL OVER THE WORLD.

MEGA MOUTHS

UNDERWATER ROAR

Underwater, a blue whale's whistle can be heard 500 miles (800 km) away. That's as loud as a supertanker.

= 188 dB

BOOMING BIGMOUTH

The noisiest animal for its size is the tiny European water boatman. Underwater, it's as loud as a chamber orchestra.

= 105 dB

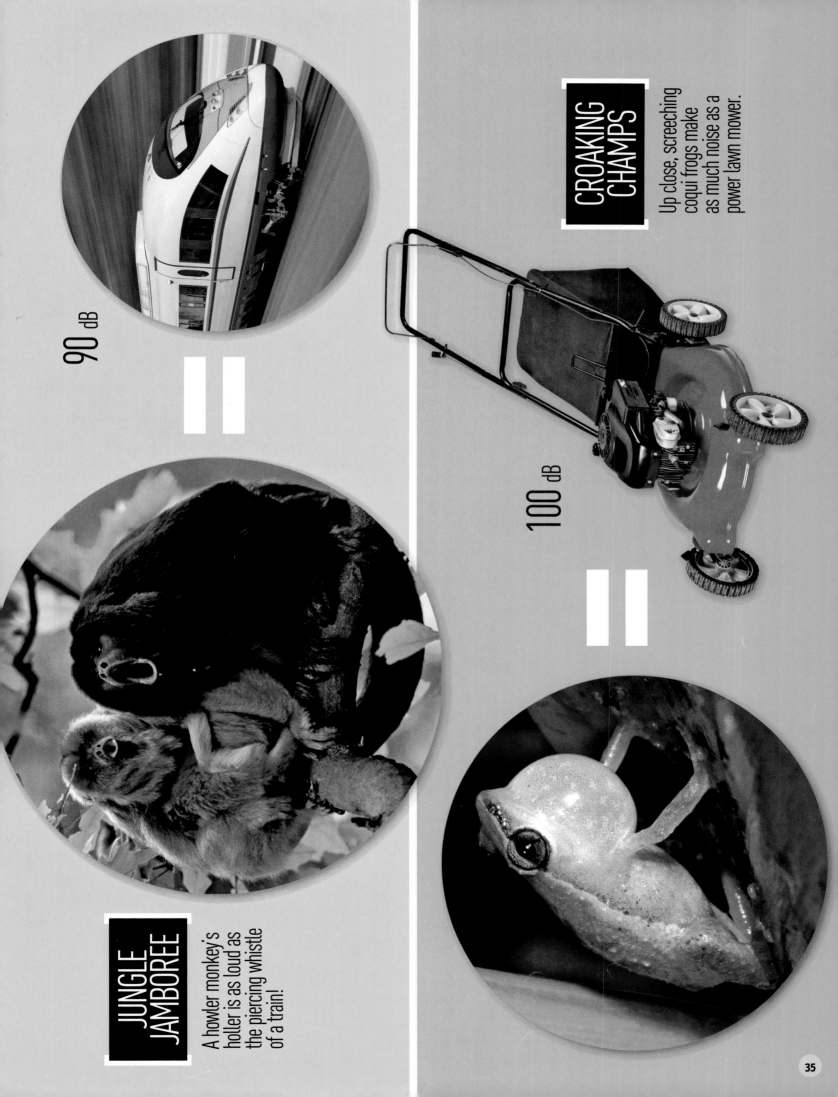

90 dB

=

JUNGLE JAMBOREE

A howler monkey's holler is as loud as the piercing whistle of a train!

=

100 dB

CROAKING CHAMPS

Up close, screeching coqui frogs make as much noise as a power lawn mower.

35

IN 2014, AIRLINES **CANCELED** **112 FLIGHTS** TO AVOID HITTING THE LANTERNS.

THE LANTERNS **SYMBOLIZE WORRIES** AND PROBLEMS **FLOATING AWAY**, THEREBY BRINGING **GOOD LUCK.**

EVERY YEAR MORE THAN **10,000** LANTERNS— **TALL** SOME AS **TALL** AS **55 INCHES**— (140 CM) FLOAT UP INTO THE NIGHT SKY AT A **FESTIVAL** IN THAILAND.

FOR OVER **700 YEARS,** THE **LANNA PEOPLE** OF NORTHERN THAILAND HAVE CELEBRATED YI PENG WITH THIS FESTIVAL OF **LIGHTS.**

9 HAIR-

THE **WORLD'S LARGEST AFRO** MEASURED MORE THAN **4 FEET** AROUND. (1.2 M)

A man pulled a **21,132-pound** (9,585 kg) **BUS** using his **HAIR.**

TO CLEAN UP AFTER AN **OiL SPiLL,** **CREWS** USED **STOCKINGS** STUFFED WITH **HUMAN HAIR.**

The world's tallest mohawk was just over **44 inches** high. (112 cm)

RAISING FACTS

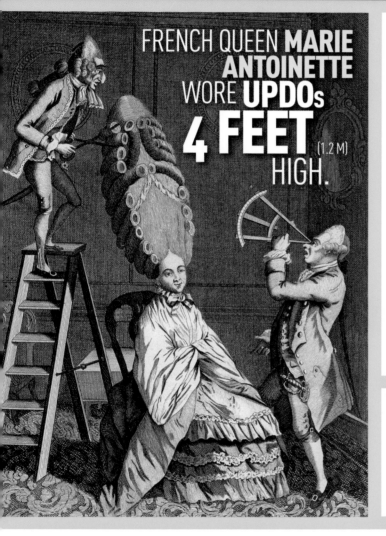

FRENCH QUEEN **MARIE ANTOINETTE** WORE **UPDO**s **4 FEET** (1.2 M) HIGH.

MIAO WOMEN IN CHINA WEAR **HORNS** WRAPPED IN THEIR **ANCESTORS' HAIR.**

A LOCK OF **ELVIS'S HAIR** SOLD AT AUCTION FOR **$115,000.**

DOCTORS REMOVED A **HAIR BALL** THE SIZE OF A **BASKETBALL** FROM A TIGER.

A CHINESE MAN HOLDS THE RECORD FOR THE **WORLD'S LONGEST HAIR (18.5 FEET).** (5.6 M)

MonsterWheel

IN LAS VEGAS, U.S.A., YOU CAN TAKE A SPIN ON THE WORLD'S BIGGEST **HIGH ROLLER!**

Each of the **28 PODS** weighs about **44,000 POUNDS** (19,960 kg).

The **HIGH ROLLER** IS **550 FEET** (168 m) high—**100 FEET** (32.5 m) **TALLER** than the **LONDON EYE.**

The **AXLE**, the largest piece of steel **EVER FORGED** in the United States, weighs **46.5 TONS** (42 t).

EACH CABLE can take the **WEIGHT** of **550 TONS** (499 t). That's equal to the weight of **100 ELEPHANTS!**

1,120 PEOPLE can RIDE the WHEEL at once.

The different parts of the wheel were made IN CHINA, JAPAN, FRANCE, SWEDEN, ITALY, THE NETHERLANDS, GERMANY, and the U.S.A.

It NEVER stops MOVING! The wheel travels about 10.5 INCHES (26.5 cm) PER SECOND.

SEVEN WEDDINGS took place on the wheel within the FIRST 100 DAYS of its OPENING.

2,000 sparkling LED LIGHTS illuminate the wheel AT NIGHT.

The wheel contains 7.2 MILLION POUNDS (3.3 million kg) of STEEL.

Wacky Duck

∧∧∧ **WHERE IS IT?**
Long Island, New York, U.S.A.

∧ **WHY IT'S WILD:**
The Big Duck houses duck-themed
souvenirs. Its **eyes** are taillights from
a Ford Model T, one of America's first cars.

≪≪≪
WHERE IS IT?
Jabiru, Australia

WHY IT'S WILD:
The Kakadu Crocodile **hotel**
serves Australia's largest national
park, a protected area with
10,000 crocs.

Crocodile Inn

Buildings Shaped Like
ANiMALS

WHERE IS IT?
Hyderabad, India

∨∨∨ **WHY IT'S WILD:**
The building may be zany, but **fishing**
is a **hot topic** at the National
Fisheries Development Board.

Fishy Business

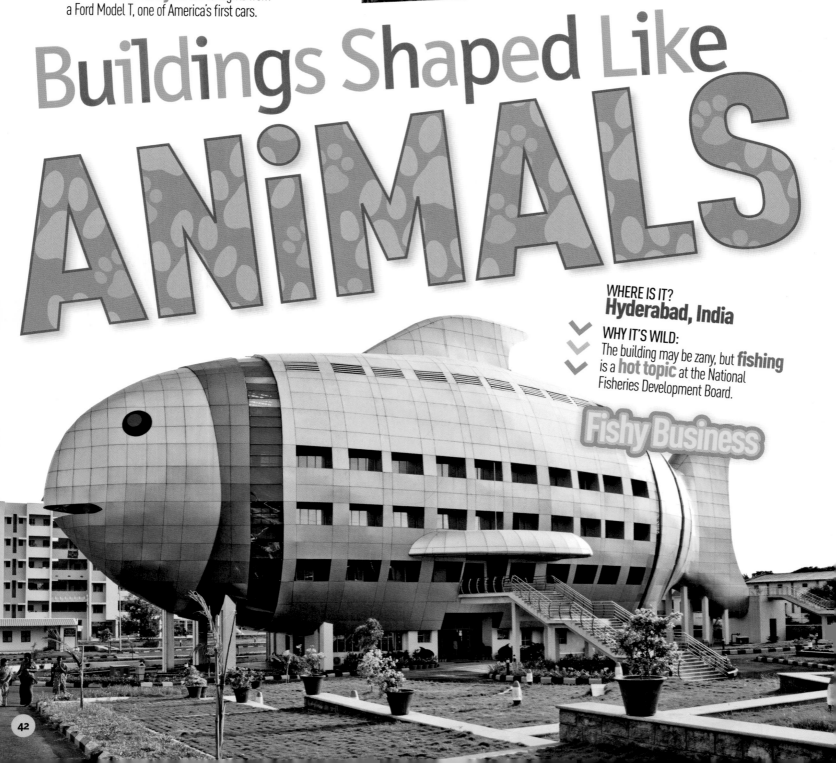

Shop in a Sheep

^ ^ ^ **WHERE IS IT?**
Tirau, New Zealand

WHY IT'S WILD:
Although it's shaped like a sheep, here the **wool** is on the inside! You can buy all sorts of fluffy things at this sheep-shaped **shop.**

Quirky Turtle

^ ^ ^ **WHERE IS IT?**
Java, Indonesia

WHY IT'S WILD:
This giant turtle lounges on the edge of tourist hot spot Kartini Beach. Inside, real sea turtles **swim** around in the big **aquarium.**

Tall Tusker

^ ^ ^ **WHERE IS IT?**
Margate City, New Jersey, U.S.A.

WHY IT'S WILD:
Lucy the Elephant, built in 1881, was the **first animal-shaped building** in North America. Visitors can tour inside, where a spiral **staircase** leads right to the top.

43

SOME SALTWATER

CROCODILES

CAN GROW UP TO
22 FEET LONG.
(6.7 M)

THAT'S ABOUT AS LONG AS ...

9 skateboards

14 dachshunds

22 submarine sandwiches

THAT'S ALMOST 2 FEET LONGER (0.6 M) THAN A PICKUP TRUCK.

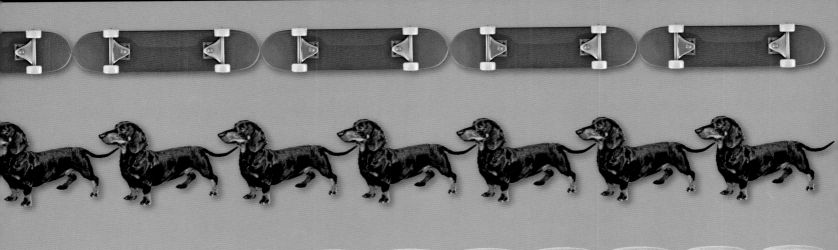

Pandas eat a lot of bamboo and their throats have a special lining to protect them from splinters! Find out more cool facts about pandas on page 48.

Giant pandas have **black skin** under their **black fur** and **pink skin** under the **white.**

CHAPTER 3

TAKE A NUMBER

PANDA-monium!

FastFACTS

WHAT: Papier-mâché pandas

HOW MANY: 1,600

WHY: To help the World Wildlife Fund (WWF) raise awareness of the panda's endangered status, the animal appears in the WWF logo

WHERE MADE: Hong Kong

WHO MADE THEM: French sculptor Paulo Grangeon

MATERIAL: Papier-mâché

THE PAPIER-MÂCHÉ PANDAS' GLOBAL TOUR COINCIDED WITH THE 50TH ANNIVERSARY OF THE WWF.

PAPIER-MÂCHÉ MEANS "CHEWED PAPER" IN FRENCH, BUT THE FRENCH DIDN'T INVENT THIS TECHNIQUE—IT STARTED IN CHINA!

There are just **1,600** pandas living in the wild. To spread the word, 1,600 **papier-mâché pandas** toured **100 cities** around the world.

THE TRAVELING PANDAS TOURED MORE THAN 100 LOCATIONS, INCLUDING PARIS, BERLIN, AND HONG KONG (PICTURED). GOOD THING THEY DON'T GET JET LAG!

Pandas in DANGER

The giant panda is the rarest member of the bear family and one of the world's most endangered species.

Pandas live in the mountain forests of central China.

Bamboo makes up 99 percent of a panda's diet! A panda needs to eat 84 pounds (38 kg) of bamboo each day to get the nutrition it needs.

THE PANDAS COME IN SIX DIFFERENT SIZES AND POSES.

THE SCULPTOR MADE A CLAY MODEL OF EACH DESIGN. THESE WERE USED TO MAKE PLASTER MOLDS AND VOLUNTEERS FINISHED THE PANDAS BY HAND.

9 COOL

THE DOLLAR SYMBOL APPEARED ON U.S. CURRENCY FOR THE **FiRST** TIME IN 2007—ON A **DOLLAR COIN.**

There are two ATMs in **ANTARCTICA.**

ONE-THIRD OF ALL U.S. CURRENCY WAS **COUNTERFEIT** BY THE END OF THE **CiViL WAR.**

IT IS **ILLEGAL** FOR TRAVELERS TO TAKE **MORE THAN $5** IN **PENNIES OUT OF THE UNITED STATES.**

IN 2009, **Zimbabwe** ISSUED A **one-hundred-TRILLiON-dollar** BANKNOTE.

FACTS ABOUT CASH

CUSTOMS POLICE TRAIN DOGS TO SNiFF OUT COUNTERFEIT CASH at BORDER CROSSINGS.

A MAN IN CALIFORNIA, U.S.A., HAS 1,497 ACTIVE CREDIT CARDS. HE'S KNOWN AS Mr. Plastic Fantastic.

ONLY 8% OF THE WORLD'S CURRENCY EXISTS AS CASH. THE REST IS ELECTRONIC.

IT WAS WORTH JUST U.S. $300.

DURING THE GREAT DEPRESSION OF THE 1930s, PEOPLE IN TENINO, WASHINGTON, U.S.A., MADE WOODEN MONEY.

THERE ARE 169,518,829,100,544,000,000,000,000 WAYS TO PLAY THE **FIRST TEN MOVES** IN A **GAME OF CHESS.**

THE LONGEST EVER GAME OF **MONOPOLY** LASTED 70 DAYS.

IF YOU TURNED A **RUBiK'S CUBE** ONCE EVERY SECOND, IT WOULD TAKE YOU **137** **TRILLION YEARS** TO WORK THROUGH ALL THE **DIFFERENT COMBINATIONS.**

SONiC THE **HEDGEHOG** CAN RUN AT THE **SPEED OF SOUND—** **768** MILES AN HOUR (1,236 KPH).

IN **SCRABBLE,** THE WORD **CAZiQUES** SCORED A RECORD **392** POINTS IN A SINGLE TURN.

THERE ARE

2,598,960
FiVE-CARD HANDS POSSIBLE IN A DECK OF **PLAYING CARDS.**

ALL THE
SCRABBLE
TiLES
EVER MADE COULD CIRCLE THE EARTH
8 TiMES.

THE FiRST
CANDY
LAND
GAMES
SOLD FOR
JUST
$1
iN 1949.

THE PROBABILITY OF ROLLING A
YAHTZEE
IN ONE ROLL IS **1 IN 1,296.**

ONE TYPE OF **POKÉMON** HAS
4,294,967,296
UNIQUE SPOT PATTERNS.

A KOALA SLEEPS

for up to **22 HOURS** per day.

While it's SNOOZING ...

YOU COULD WATCH AT LEAST 11 MOVIES.

RUNNERS COULD COMPLETE 10 MARATHONS ONE AFTER THE OTHER—THAT'S 264 MILES (425 KM).

YOU COULD FLY FROM SAN FRANCISCO TO LONDON ... AND BACK AGAIN!

CRAYOLA COULD MAKE 11 MILLION CRAYONS.

TOP-DOLLAR
Bling

AT 30 TIMES THE PRICE OF AN **ORDINARY XBOX,** THIS **GOLD-PLATED** CONSOLE ADDS A TOUCH OF **LUXURY** TO **HOME ENTERTAINMENT.**

<<< THERE ARE 1,600 **DIAMONDS** IN THIS **$3.2 MILLION** COLLAR. THAT'S ONE PAMPERED POOCH!

>>> THIS **GOLDEN RIDE** IS YOURS FOR JUST UNDER **$5 MILLION.** EVEN THE **WATER BOTTLE** GETS THE 24-CARAT TREATMENT!

THIS **DIAMOND-ENCRUSTED**
SOCCER BALL WILL KICK A
$2.6 MILLION HOLE
IN YOUR WALLET.

AT AUCTION,
THIS
CRYSTAL PIANO
FETCHED
$3.2 MILLION.
IT WAS PLAYED AT THE
**BEIJING
OLYMPICS.**
MUSIC FOR
MILLIONAIRES!

HAVE YOUR
GOLD AND **EAT IT,** TOO!
THIS **$1,600 EDIBLE GOLD- AND
DIAMOND-COVERED DONUT**
IS FILLED WITH
CHAMPAGNE JELLY.

THIS **SHIMMERING** DESIGNER GOWN
WAS INSPIRED BY AN ICE-CREAM BAR. IT'S
DECORATED WITH 10,000 GOLD SEQUINS.

In just 1 HOUR the SUN produces more energy than the whole WORLD generates in 1 YEAR.

It takes *100,000 YEARS* for heat from the **SUN'S CORE** to make it to its OUTER LAYER, but only

8.3 MINUTES

for sunlight to reach the **EARTH.**

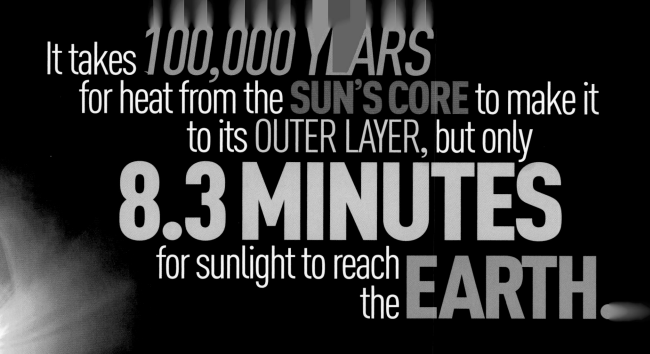

ultimate secret revealed!

How does the sun make all this energy?

Our sun is massive—roughly as big as one million Earths. This huge ball of fire burns 700 million tons (635 million t) of hydrogen in its core every second. About five million tons of that hydrogen converts to pure energy in that time! Every year, the Earth absorbs 94 billion megawatts of energy from the sun, and this radiates back as heat. Scientists are currently investigating ways of using the sun's energy to power our world. You may have seen solar panels on buildings. Their photovoltaic, or solar, cells convert sunlight to electricity. And, as long as the sun keeps shining—at least for the next several billion years—we are sure to discover more ways to use its amazing energy!

9 MIND-BOGGLING

IN A ROOM OF **JUST** 23 PEOPLE, THERE IS A 50 PERCENT CHANCE THAT **2 PEOPLE** WILL HAVE THE SAME **BIRTHDAY.**

MULTIPLY **1,089 × 9,** AND YOU GET THE E×ACT REVERSE: **9,801.**

AN **iCOSAHEDRON** HAS **20 SiDES.** IT'S BEEN USED FOR **DiCE** SINCE ANCIENT EGYPTIAN TIMES.

IN **JAPAN,** THEY HAVE **CONTESTS** TO SEE HOW FAST **KIDS** CAN ADD USING AN **ABACUS.**

MATH FACTS

THE **EGYPTIAN HEIROGLYPH** FOR
100,000
WAS A
FROG.

ZERO IS THE **ONLY** NUMBER THAT **CANNOT** BE REPRESENTED IN **ROMAN NUMERALS.**

THE **NUMBERS** WE WRITE WITH TODAY WERE **INVENTED IN INDIA**
2,000 YEARS AGO.

IN **QATAR,** THE CELL PHONE NUMBER
666-6666
SOLD FOR **$2.7 MILLION!**

CROWS
can be trained to
COUNT ALOUD.

Prime Survival

COULD **CICADAS** BE **MATH CHAMPS?**
THEIR LIFE CYCLES REVEAL AWESOME **NUMERICAL PATTERNS,** SO MATH IS **WIRED** INTO THEIR **DNA.**

THE CICADA is one of the world's **LONGEST-LIVING INSECTS.**

PRIME NUMBERS, like **13** and **17,** are only **DIVISIBLE BY THEMSELVES** and **1.**

PERIODICAL CICADAS spend **13** or **17 YEARS UNDERGROUND.**

MALE cicadas sing louder than **100 DECIBELS—** as loud as a **LAWN MOWER.**

3 SPECIES of cicada appear every **17 YEARS** and **4 SPECIES** every **13 YEARS.**

Cicadas that **EMERGE** in **DIFFERENT YEARS** often do **NOT SURVIVE.**

The **TRANSPARENT** wings of **CICADAS FILTER OUT ULTRAVIOLET** light.

SAFETY in numbers! **MILLIONS** of cicadas **SURFACE AT ONCE** to **MATE** and **LAY EGGS.**

Cicadas **DIE A FEW WEEKS** after coming to the **SURFACE.**

EACH FEMALE lays **400–600 EGGS.**

YUM! Cicadas suck **SAP** from **TREE ROOTS.**

More than **150 BiLLiON** pennies are in circulation. That's **MORE** than **ALL** the nickels, dimes, and quarters COMBINED.

Lined up, all those pennies would stretch

144,469 MiLES—

(232,500 km)

more than **halfway** to the

moon.

ultimate secret revealed!

When will the penny drop? It may be surprising to discover that the cost of making one cent is higher than the coin itself is worth. In fact, each penny costs 1.8 cents to produce. This is because the metals from which the coins are made—copper and zinc—have become expensive in recent years. There have been calls to make the coins from cheaper metals, such as steel, or to eliminate them from U.S. currency altogether. But the pretty penny is a popular coin, so it looks set to stay a while longer.

There are also **buildings** shaped like **footballs**, **baskets**, and even **animals!**

This bulky bulldozer is actually home to a construction company in California, U.S.A.

CHAPTER 4

WaCkY WORLD

SCiENCE ON STiLTS

The futuristic-looking **Halley VI** is the **first** of its kind—a fully **movable** research station in the Antarctic **deep freeze.**

British Antarctic Survey

NATURAL ENVIRONMENT RESEARCH COUNCIL

FOUR FEET (1.2 M) OF SNOW ACCUMULATES EACH YEAR ON ANTARCTICA'S BRUNT ICE SHELF.

TEMPERATURES CAN DROP TO -58°F (-50°C) IN WINTER. THE 100-MILE-AN-HOUR (161-KPH) WINDS DRIVE COLD, SHARP ICE PARTICLES ACROSS THE LANDSCAPE.

FastFACTS

WHAT: Halley VI—an 8-module research station

WHY: Scientists needed a movable station from which to gather atmospheric data

WHERE: Brunt Ice Shelf, Antarctica

WHEN: Since February 2012

WHO: British Antarctic Survey; Hugh Broughton, architect

MOST WORK IS CARRIED OUT BY A 70-STRONG TEAM DURING THE SUMMER MONTHS. A SMALL TEAM OF 16 STAYS IN WINTER TO KEEP PROGRAMS RUNNING.

Skiing to SAFETY

There have been research stations at Halley since 1956, but most have been crushed or buried by accumulating snow. Halley VI's stilts stand on skis, which means it can move to a new location whenever the snow builds up!

THE STATION IS MADE OF MODULES. SEVEN ARE BLUE. THE EIGHTH, A RED MODULE, CONTAINS A COMMON LIVING AREA, KITCHEN, AND GYM.

DATA COLLECTED HERE HELPS SCIENTISTS LEARN MORE ABOUT THE OZONE AND RISING SEA LEVELS.

THE NEAREST SETTLEMENT IS ABOUT 1,118 MILES (1,800 KM) AWAY.

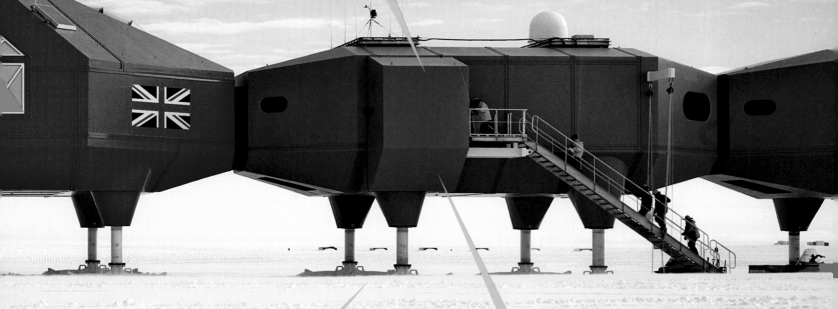

THE ICE BENEATH THE STATION MOVES AT A RATE OF OVER 1,300 FEET (400 M) A YEAR.

IT TOOK FOUR YEARS AND ALMOST $42 MILLION TO BUILD HALLEY VI.

Wacky

ROADSIDE SIGHTS

HOP ABOARD A BUS AT THIS **WATERMELON,** ONE OF **16 FRUIT-SHAPED** BUS STOPS IN KONAGAI, JAPAN.

THE WORLD'S LARGEST **EASTER EGG** IN ALBERTA, CANADA, IS MADE OF OVER **3,500** ALUMINUM PIECES AND WEIGHS A HEFTY **5,000** POUNDS. (2,268 KG).

THIS 20-FOOT-HIGH (6-M) **WHALE** IN OKLAHOMA, U.S.A., IS BEACHED OFF THE FAMOUS **ROUTE 66.**

A 26-FOOT-TALL (8-M)
TREE SCULPTURE >>>
IN LONDON, ENGLAND, HAS
75 SETS
OF RANDOMLY FLASHING
TRAFFIC LIGHTS.

THIS SUPERSIZE
BULLDOZER
IS THE OFFICE
BUILDING
OF A CALIFORNIA, U.S.A.,
COMPANY THAT MAKES
CONSTRUCTION EQUIPMENT.

(6.5-M) SLICE
THIS 21-FOOT
PROUDLY REPRESENTS
NEW ZEALAND'S
KIWIFRUIT -GROWING REGION.

A BODY OF WATER LIES DEEP BELOW THE EARTH'S SURFACE—IT'S **THREE TIMES LARGER** THAN **ALL** EARTH'S OCEANS PUT TOGETHER.

CAVE CAVE CAVE

THOUSANDS OF GLOWWORMS LOOK LIKE A STARRY SKY IN A **NEW ZEALAND**

THE GREAT BLUE **HOLE**

NEAR **BELIZE** IS AN UNDERWATER SINKHOLE 480 feet (146.3 m) DEEP.

YOU CAN RIDE A **FERRIS** WHEEL UNDERGROUND iN ROMANiA

A CALIFORNIA, U.S.A., COUPLE ONCE FOUND $10,000 WORTH OF **GOLD** IN THFIR **BACKYARD**

A MOUNTAIN VAULT IN NORWAY STORES

740,000 SEED SAMPLES.

A CATHEDRAL WAS BUILT **443 feet** (135 m) **DEEP** IN A **POLISH** SALT MINE.

AFTER A FIRE IN 1889, BUILDERS MADE THE STREETS IN SEATTLE, U.S.A., UP TO **30 FEET** (9 M) HIGHER. TODAY YOU CAN TOUR PART OF THE OLD CITY UNDERGROUND.

OVER 2,000 YEARS AGO PEOPLE IN **CAPPADOCIA, TURKEY,** LIVED INSIDE **TOWERS OF ROCK!**

ABOUT **3,500 PEOPLE** LIVE IN **UNDERGROUND** DUGOUTS IN COOBER PEDY, AUSTRALIA.

WHERE IS IT?
Papua New Guinea

WHY IT'S COOL:
The **Korowai people** build houses on stilts up to **115 feet** (35 m) from the ground, to protect them from rival tribes.

TREE-TOPPING Houses

Rain Forest Rooftop
^^

WHERE IS IT?
Near La Gamba, Costa Rica

WHY IT'S COOL:
People can **live** in this treetop community all year round. They get about using walkways and **zip lines** from tree to tree.

WHERE IS IT?
Auckland, New Zealand

WHY IT'S COOL:
This cocoon-shaped **party pod** is 33 feet (10 m) wide and made from pine and poplar.

Eat With the Birds
>>>

House of Mirrors

> **WHERE IS IT?**
> **Harads, Sweden**

> **WHY IT'S COOL:**
> The **Mirrorcube** cabin seems to disappear into the woods. **Infrared film** covers the outside walls. Visible only to birds, it stops them from crashing into the building!

> **WHERE IS IT?**
> **British Columbia, Canada**

> **WHY IT'S COOL:**
> Three houses in one nestle in the **Enchanted Forest** adventure park. The highest is 47 feet (14 m) up, at the top of 64 winding **steps.**

Fairy-Tale Forest

> **WHERE IS IT?**
> **Okinawa, Japan**

> **WHY IT'S COOL:**
> This tree looks like the local **banyan** tree, but is made of **concrete.** At the top, the Gajumaru restaurant sits 20 feet (6 m) above the town.

City View

AT OVER

50 feet (15 m) **LONG**

AND

20 feet (6 m) **HIGH**

SPINOSAURUS WAS THE **BIGGEST, BADDEST MEAT-EATER** that **ever lived.**

SPINOSAURUS WAS ALMOST **10 FEET** (3 M) BIGGER THAN *T. REX!*

SPINOSAURUS LIVED ABOUT **112** TO **97 MILLION** YEARS AGO.

THIS FIERCE FISH-EATER HAD A LONG, CROCODILE-SHAPED MOUTH—PERFECT FOR EATING **CAR-SIZE** PREHISTORIC FISH LIKE THE COELACANTH IN **ONE BITE.**

MASSIVE **7-FOOT** (2-M) **SPINES** COVERED IN SKIN MADE A **SAIL** ON ITS **BACK.**

SPINOSAURUS MEANS "**SPINE LIZARD.**"

SPINOSAURUS IS THE ONLY KNOWN **SWIMMING** DINOSAUR.

8 WACKY

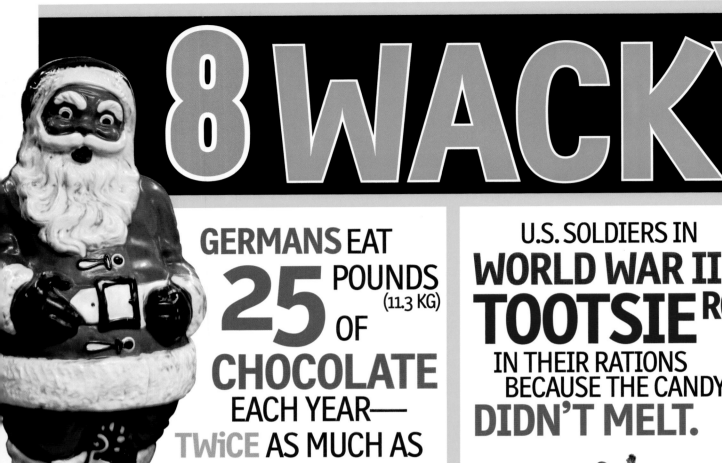

GERMANS EAT **25** POUNDS (11.3 KG) OF **CHOCOLATE** EACH YEAR— **TWICE** AS MUCH AS **AMERICANS.**

U.S. SOLDIERS IN **WORLD WAR II** GOT **TOOTSIE** ROLLS IN THEIR RATIONS BECAUSE THE CANDY **DIDN'T MELT.**

BUBBLE GUM IS **PINK** BECAUSE ITS *INVENTOR* HAD NO OTHER **COLOR** ON HAND WHEN MAKING IT.

IN 1953, IT TOOK 27 HOURS TO MAKE A **PEEP.** TODAY, IT TAKES JUST **6 MINUTES.**

200 MILLION

FACTS ABOUT CANDY

BRIGHT-COLORED **SUGAR SKULLS** DECORATE ALTARS ON **THE DAY OF THE DEAD** IN MEXICO.

LAID **END** TO **END**, ALL THE **CANDY CORN** MADE EACH YEAR WOULD CIRCLE THE WORLD **5.7** TIMES.

COTTON CANDY WAS INVENTED BY A **DENTiST** IN **1897.**

SKITTLES ARE MADE EVERY DAY.

PROBLEM

I Spy

‹‹‹
In 1945, the Russians gave the U.S. ambassador a very special replica of the Great Seal of the United States—one incorporating a hidden microphone! For six years during the Cold War (when U.S. relations with Russia were decidedly frosty), the seal hung at the ambassador's home in Moscow, letting the Russians listen in.

Presents

THESE GIFTS WEREN'T ON ANYONE'S LIST!
SOME CAME FROM SNEAKY SPIES AND SOLDIERS. OTHERS CAME FROM GENEROUS PEOPLE WHOSE GIFT **MISSED THE MARK.**

Sneak Attack

During the Trojan War, the ancient Greeks feigned defeat and sailed away. They left a giant wooden horse behind, which the Trojans took as a trophy. At night Greek soldiers jumped out of the horse and attacked. Surprise!

›››

‹‹‹
Pile of Old Stones

In 1915, Sir Cecil Chubb bought Stonehenge on a whim at auction—some say, as a gift for his wife. He gave the monument to Britain three years later.

>>> Old Thai Trick

Long ago, kings in Thailand would give a sacred white elephant to people they really didn't like. These big gifts cost so much to keep that the unlucky recipient often ended up penniless!

Nowhere to Stand

When France gave the United States the Statue of Liberty in 1886, there was just one problem—the statue had no pedestal. To get Lady Liberty standing, Americans had to raise $100,000—over $2 million in today's money!

^ Fit for a Prince?

Liberian President Tubman gave a pair of pygmy hippos to Britain's Prince Philip in 1961. Unfortunately, there was no place to keep the hippos in the palace, so the prince found them a new home in a zoo.

ANT COLONIES CAN LIVE AS **DEEP** AS **20 FEET** (6 M) UNDERGROUND.

HONEYPOT ANTS ARE **EDIBLE** AND ARE SOMETIMES **EATEN** IN **AUSTRALIA**.

THERE ARE **MORE** THAN **TEN QUADRILLION** ANTS IN THE **WORLD** (THAT'S 10,000,000,000,000,000!).

HONEYPOT WORKER ANTS, WHICH STORE NECTAR IN THEIR BODIES, CAN SWELL TO THE SIZE OF A CHERRY TOMATO.

WHO: Rusco the Chihuahua

WHY HE'S TALENTED: This Californian rescue dog starred as Papi in the *Beverly Hills Chihuahua* trilogy. He learned his **stunts** for the first movie in just six months.

WHO: Snowball the Cockatoo

WHY HE'S TALENTED: Sulphur-crested Snowball became an Internet **sensation** with his dance moves. The **cockatoo's** amazing talents landed him spots in TV commercials.

ANiMALS
Have Talent

WHO: Metro the Horse

WHY HE'S TALENTED: Metro retired from **racing** and took up a **paintbrush!** Half the money he makes on his art helps care for other retired racehorses.

Painting Pony

>>>
Ocean Rescue

WHO:
Winter the Dolphin

WHY SHE'S TALENTED:
The star of *Dolphin Tale,* a movie about her life, Winter got caught in a crab trap, where she lost her tail. Today, she swims with a **prosthetic tail** and inspires kids with disabilities.

<<<
Dancing Dog

WHO:
Pudsey the Pooch

WHY HE'S TALENTED:
After winning a TV talent show dancing with his **trainer,** Ashleigh, this cute canine went on to star in his own **Hollywood movie.**

WHO:
Eddie the Sea Otter

WHY HE'S TALENTED:
Eddie **shoots hoops** in his pool at Oregon Zoo, U.S.A. Eddie is 15 years old and the exercise helps ease his **arthritic elbow.**

Hoop Star

In 1869, a Frenchman designed an early version of this wacky wheel, using bicycle parts. Check out page 90 for other mind-bending inventions!

CHAPTER 5

StRANGE SMaRTS

The BRAIN is 60% fat.

It's the fattiest organ in the body.

Every day between 50,000 and 70,000 THOUGHTS whiz through the brain.

ultimate secret revealed!

Doesn't the fat slow the brain down?

No way! Inside your brain, information travels at up to 268 miles an hour (431 kph)—faster than a passenger train. Messages zip from one brain cell to another along nerve fibers wrapped in a protective membrane mostly made of fat. The fat insulates the fibers and actually increases the speed at which information travels. When you learn something new, the fibers connect one brain cell to others using tiny branches. You have more of these connections in your brain than there are galaxies in the universe. It's mind-blowing!

CRAZY iNVENTiONS

MEET **LITTERFISH**— THE PERFECT ANSWER WHEN KITTY NEEDS A LITTLE **PRIVACY.** THE PULL-OUT LITTER TRAY MAKES IT ⌄⌄⌄ A CINCH TO **CLEAN.**

ROLL ON, ⌃⌃⌃ BUT DON'T FALL OFF! THERE'S NO STEERING WHEEL ON THIS **MOTORIZED MONOCYCLE**— IT'S ALL ABOUT **BALANCE!**

EVEN A **BABY** >>> **CAN CLEAN THE FLOOR**—IF HE'S WEARING THIS **MOP-FITTED ONESIE.**

>>> THIS **NIFTY GADGET** USES **WOODEN PADS** AND **VACUUM CLEANER** TECHNOLOGY TO TURN ITS INVENTOR INTO A WALL-SCALING SPIDER-BOY.

YOUR DOG COULD BE **TOAST**! SELFIE >>> TOASTERS USE A SPECIAL INSERT THAT TOASTS THE IMAGE OF YOUR CHOICE ONTO **A SLICE OF BREAD.**

RUNNY NOSE? THIS **JAPANESE INVENTION** PROVIDES A CONSTANT SUPPLY OF <<< TISSUE ... UNTIL THE ROLL RUNS OUT, THAT IS.

The BRAINY **weaverbird** is the only bird that can TIE KNOTS.

→ It builds its nest using dozens of different knots and loops— even while hanging upside down!

→ The bird can also judge how tight to pull on a strip of grass before it will snap.

→ Male birds often build several nests, and the female picks her favorite.

→ Weavers are quick learners, making a better nest every time.

→ Sociable weavers build nests that weigh over 2,000 pounds [907 kg] and house over 100 mini-nests inside.

9 Incredible

A MEDIUM-SIZE **CUMULUS CLOUD** WEIGHS ABOUT THE SAME AS **80** ELEPHANTS.

A RADAR ENGINEER **INVENTED** THE **MICROWAVE** AFTER HE NOTICED THAT **ENERGY WAVES** COULD MELT A CANDY BAR IN HIS POCKET.

YOUR HAND IS **HOT** ENOUGH TO **MELT** THE METAL **GALLIUM.**

There are **100 billion galaxies** in the universe. We can see only **5** of them with the naked eye.

FACTS ABOUT SCIENCE

There are enough **CARBON ATOMS** in the human body TO MAKE ABOUT **9,000 PENCILS.**

STARLIGHT COLORS THE UNIVERSE **BEIGE-WHITE.** ASTRONOMERS CALL IT **"COSMIC LATTE."**

3-D DOCTORS USED A PRINTER TO MAKE A **PLASTIC SKULL** FOR A **PATIENT.**

THE **OCEANS** CONTAIN ENOUGH **SALT** TO COVER EARTH'S LANDMASSES **COMPLETELY.** THE SALT LAYER WOULD BE NEARLY **500 feet** (152 m) **deep.**

ALL THE **MATTER** THAT MAKES UP THE **HUMAN RACE** COULD FIT INTO A **SUGAR CUBE.**

ATOMS ARE **99.99999999999999** PERCENT EMPTY SPACE.

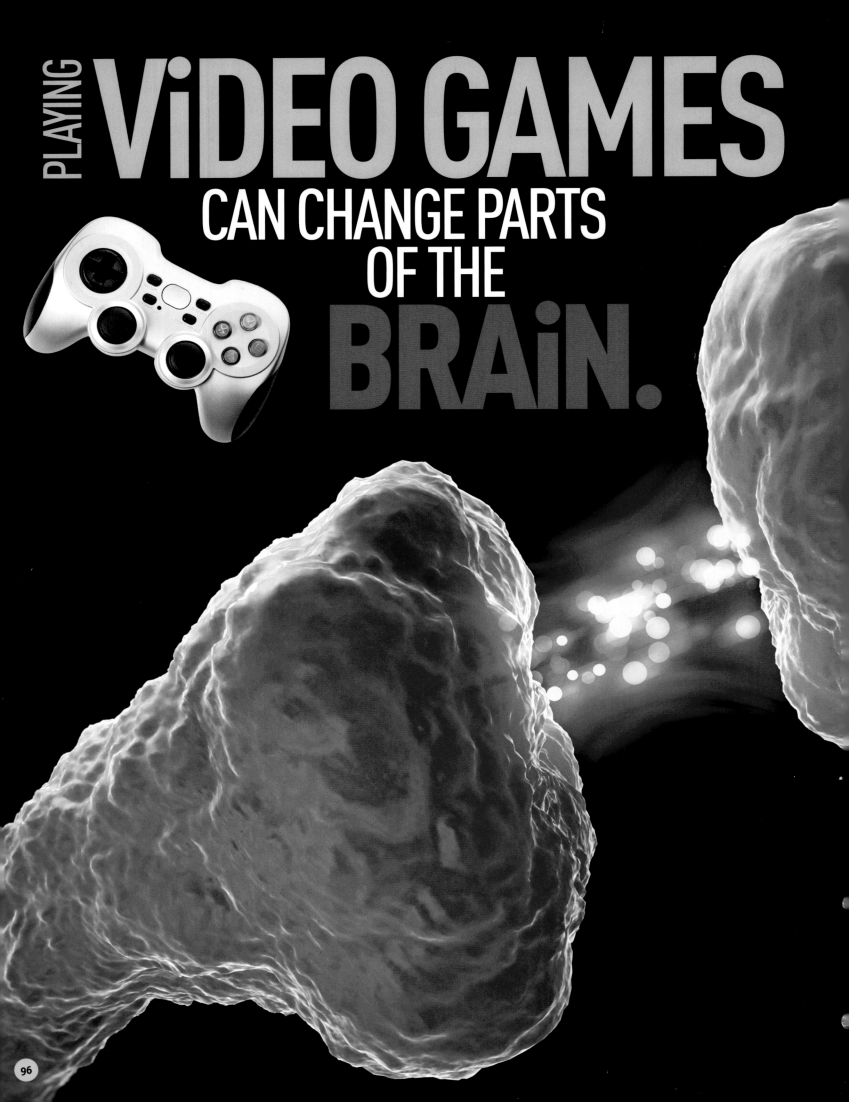

PLAYING ViDEO GAMES CAN CHANGE PARTS OF THE BRAiN.

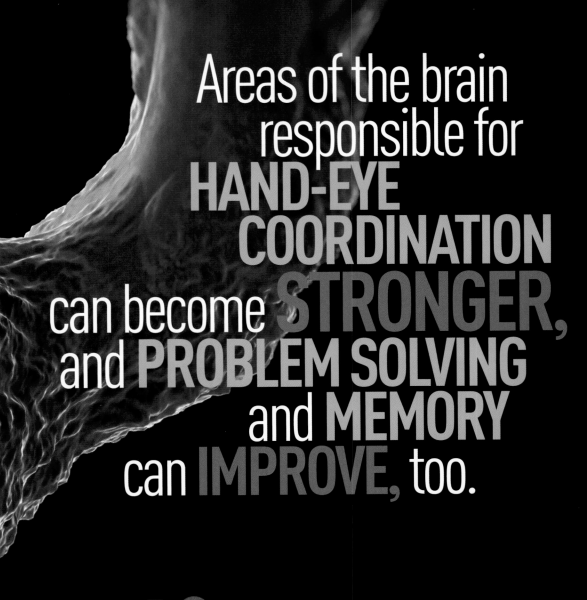

Areas of the brain responsible for **HAND-EYE COORDINATION** can become **STRONGER,** and **PROBLEM SOLVING** and **MEMORY** can **IMPROVE,** too.

ultimate secret revealed!

How do we know what video games do to the brain? The billions of neurons (nerve cells) in the brain are connected by tiny branches called "synapses." These send information as electrical impulses from one neuron to the next. The more the brain practices doing something, the speedier these impulses become, and the sharper the brain grows.

ABOUT 79,100 LANGUAGES ARE SPOKEN WORLDWIDE.

2,300 OF THE WORLD'S LANGUAGES ARE SPOKEN IN ASIA.

THE WORLD'S SHORTEST ALPHABET HAS 12 LETTERS; THE LONGEST ONE HAS 74 LETTERS.

THE SOUTHERN AFRICAN N|uu LANGUAGE USES CLICKING SOUNDS FOR ITS 52 CONSONANTS.

SINCE COLUMBUS'S TIME 115 LANGUAGES HAVE BECOME EXTINCT IN THE UNITED STATES.

14.4 PERCENT OF THE **WORLD'S POPULATION** SPEAKS **MANDARIN.**

THERE ARE MORE THAN **50,000** CHARACTERS IN THE CHINESE LANGUAGE.

ENGLISH IS THE OFFICIAL LANGUAGE OF 54 COUNTRIES.

THE WORD **"SET"** HAS **464** DEFINITIONS IN THE **OXFORD ENGLISH DICTIONARY.**

Check out these six **wacky** creations from the **robotics lab.**

Military Marvel

An army prototype, **BigDog** is a pack animal that never tires! It can tackle the roughest terrain carrying a whopping **340-pound** (154-kg) load.

<<<

ROBOTS IN ACTION

Robot Cop

>>>

At **8 feet** (2.4 m) tall, this **solar-powered traffic** cop stands head and shoulders above the traffic in the Democratic Republic of Congo. It even **tells** pedestrians when it's safe to **cross.**

Bionic Man

<<<

Able to walk, talk, and **breathe,** this medical **dummy** showcases all the elements of the human body that can be rebuilt using state-of-the-art artificial **body** parts.

Easy Rider

HitchBOT spent the summer hitchhiking his way across Canada. In just 26 days and 19 vehicles, the chatty traveler rode 3,700 miles (6,000 km).

<<<

Robo Rockers

Z-Machines is no average rock band. The drummer has six arms, the guitarist has 78 fingers, and the keyboard player is wired to his instrument. They're electrifying!

Dancing Queen >>>

This all-singing, all-dancing female robot from Japan is nicknamed "Diva-bot." Computer software enables her to mimic the actions of a real performer electronically.

CELL PHONES are **400 TIMES** more **POWERFUL** than the **COMPUTER** that helped guide man to the **MOON**.

The moon has **Wi-Fi!** It comes all the way from EARTH, beamed by 4 INFRARED TELESCOPES.

ultimate secret revealed!

What do the 1969 computer used for the moon landing and your cell phone have in common? Both today's phones and the 1969 Apollo Guidance Computer (AGC) use integrated circuits, or microchips. The AGC was one of the first computers to use them. Since then, microchips keep getting smaller, but more and more powerful. The microchip inside your phone (called a SIM) runs about 30 times faster than the AGC and has about 200 times more memory—even though it's about the size of your fingernail!

WHO'S THE SMARTEST?

Scientists judge how smart a creature is by comparing **brain** size with **body** size.

WINNER!

VS

SMALL TALK

A hippo communicates using clicking sounds underwater. Meanwhile, the African gray parrot counts, recognizes colors, and talks!

VS

WINNER!

WINNER!

VS

PRACTICAL SKILLS

Horses can spot the difference between less and more with small numbers, while elephants have a complex social structure and can figure out how to use tools.

VS

LEADING LION

When it comes to hunting, a lion easily outsmarts its prey. Yet the California sea lion can understand sign language and learn to associate sounds and letters.

WINNER!

This oversize **fur-mobile** can reach a speed of **40 miles an hour—** (64 kph) but it's not road legal.

This sheep-herding pup was built in honor of this farmer's favorite sheepdog. Race over to page 118 to check out other zany vehicles.

CHAPTER 6

SpEED DeMONS

SURFING
IN THE SKY!
THIS FLYBOARD CAN SOAR
49 FEET
(15 M)

ABOVE THE
WATER.

AN ANNUAL FLYBOARD **WORLD CUP** SEES RIDERS PERFORMING AIR **SOMERSAULTS, BACKFLIPS,** AND **DIVES.**

HIGH-PRESSURE WATER POWERS THE BOARD. IT'S **PUMPED** THROUGH A **59-FOOT** (18-M) **HOSE** ATTACHED TO A **MOTORBOAT.**

JET SKI **CHAMPION FRANKY ZAPATA** DESIGNED THIS **EXTREME** SPORTS BOARD.

IN "**THREADING THE NEEDLE**" THE PERFORMER EXECUTES A **BACKFLIP** AND THEN FLIES THROUGH THE **LOOP** MADE BY THE **WATER HOSE.**

BiZARRE Races

GOAT RACING BEGAN IN **TOBAGO** 80 YEARS AGO. THE GOATS' TWO-MONTH **TRAINING PROGRAM** INCLUDES A **SWIMMING ROUTINE.**

IT TAKES A **WINNER THREE MINUTES** TO **SLIME** ITS WAY ACROSS **13 INCHES** (33 CM) OF **DAMP** CLOTH AT THE **WORLD CHAMPIONSHIP** SNAIL RACES, HELD IN THE U.K.

LAWN MOWERS TAKE TO THE TRACK IN THIS **CRAZY** GERMAN COMPETITION. ALL MOWER **BLADES** ARE REMOVED FOR **SAFETY.**

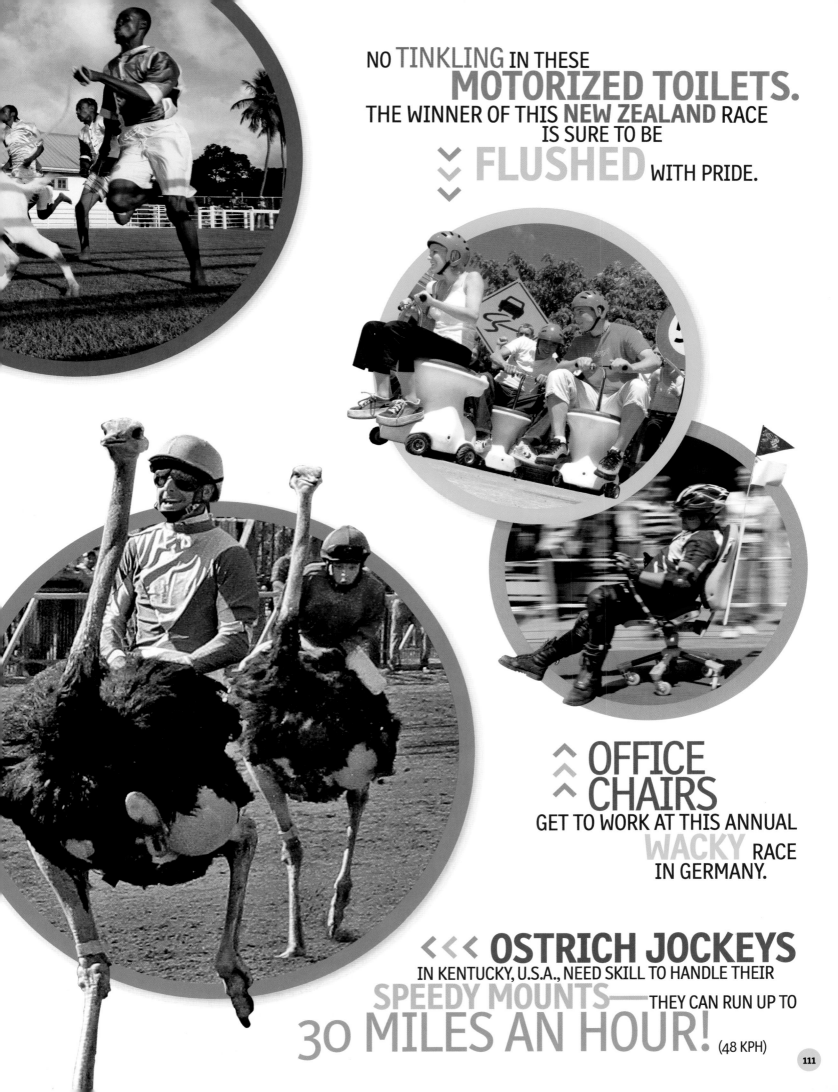

NO TINKLING IN THESE **MOTORIZED TOILETS.** THE WINNER OF THIS **NEW ZEALAND** RACE IS SURE TO BE

FLUSHED WITH PRIDE.

OFFICE CHAIRS
GET TO WORK AT THIS ANNUAL **WACKY** RACE IN GERMANY.

<<< **OSTRICH JOCKEYS**
IN KENTUCKY, U.S.A., NEED SKILL TO HANDLE THEIR **SPEEDY MOUNTS**—THEY CAN RUN UP TO **30 MILES AN HOUR!** (48 KPH)

In one hour, a **goldfish** will swim **4/5 of a mile** (1.4 km)

In that same time ...

An Olympic swimmer can swim **3.8 MILES.** (6 km)

A sea lion can swim **13.5 MILES.** (21.5 km)

A sailfish can swim **68 MILES.** (110 km)

An orca can swim **30 MILES.** (48 km)

8 DIZZYING

THE **LONGEST EVER CONGA LINE** WAS MADE UP OF **119,986** PEOPLE.

THE **TWIST** INSPIRED THE **MASHED POTATO**, THE **SWIM**, AND THE **FUNKY CHICKEN**.

A **TAP DANCER** IN **NEW YORK**, U.S.A., SET A **WORLD RECORD** FOR **MOST TAPS** IN A MINUTE— **1,163!**

A **THREE-DAY** DANCE MARATHON AT PENN STATE UNIVERSITY, U.S.A., RAISED OVER **$13 MILLION** FOR **CHARITY**.

FACTS ABOUT DANCE

FOR **19 YEARS** A **DONKEY** NAMED **MONIKA DANCED** FOR A RUSSIAN **BALLET COMPANY.**

MAY 14 IS NATIONAL CHICKEN DANCE DAY.

BALLROOMS OF THE **1920S BANNED** the **CHARLESTON** for being **TOO FAST** and **DANGEROUS.**

IN **1923,** KALAMAZOO IN MICHIGAN, U.S.A., PASSED A **LAW** AGAINST DANCERS **STARING** INTO EACH OTHER'S **EYES.**

THE AVERAGE CAR HAS 30,000 PARTS.

NiNETY PERCENT OF DRIVERS SiNG WHILE DRIVING.

AT JUST 19 INCHES HIGH, (48 CM)

THE FLATMOBILE IS THE WORLD'S LOWEST STREET-LEGAL CAR.

BLOODHOUND IS A **JET- AND ROCKET-POWERED CAR** OF THE FUTURE THAT WILL GO **1,000 MILES AN HOUR** (1,609 KPH).

AROUND THE WORLD **WHiTE** IS THE **MOST POPULAR** COLOR FOR A **NEW CAR.**

A FORMULA ONE CAR COULD DRIVE UPSIDE DOWN IN A TUNNEL, **USING THE CEILING AS A ROAD!**

SPEEDING AT **120** MILES AN HOUR (193 KPH)

OF ALL NEW CARS SOLD IN BRAZIL, 90 PERCENT USE FUEL MADE FROM SUGARCANE.

IN 2013, A **1954** MERCEDES-**BENZ** RACE CAR **SOLD FOR OVER $29 MILLION.**

2012 LAND ROVERS IN DUBAI CAME EQUIPPED WITH AN **EDIBLE** **GUIDE** ON **DESERT SURVIVAL.**

Monster Bus

> **WHAT IS IT?**
> **Charity School Bus**

> **WHY IT'S ZANY:**
> This souped-up yellow school bus is **13 feet** (4 m) tall and weighs **19,000 pounds** (8,618 kg). It's used for charity events.

Foot Power

> **WHAT IS IT?**
> **A shoe-shaped electric car**

> **WHY IT'S ZANY:**
> A Chinese company built this **leather-covered,** 10-foot (3-m)-long **car** to promote its shoes.

ZAnY Vehicles

Makeover Madness

> **WHAT IS IT?**
> **VW Revamp**

> **WHY IT'S ZANY:**
> This wacky hatchback sports more than **100 add-ons,** from **golf balls** and **flippers** to **Darth Vader** on the sunroof.

WHAT IS IT?
Giant Sheepdog

WHY IT'S ZANY:
A **farmer** in England used this **furry car,** called Floss, to round up his sheep.

Herder Instinct

Art on the Move

WHAT IS IT?:
Speed Demon

WHY IT'S ZANY:
This pedal-powered dragon **bicycle** competed in the 3-day, 42-mile (68-km) **Kinetic Sculpture Race** in California, U.S.A.

Mega Cycle

WHAT IS IT?
Junkyard Motorbike

WHY IT'S ZANY:
Six people can get a ride on this **14-foot** (4.25-m)-long **motorbike** with **tractor wheels.**

ANIMAL OLYMPICS

43 MILES AN HOUR
(69.2 KPH)

VS

RUN FOR YOUR LIFE!

At top speed, *Tyrannosaurus rex* could beat a racehorse by a nose!

WINNER!

45 MILES AN HOUR
(72.4 KPH)

LONG JUMP

The kangaroo rat could jump clean over a sleeping Bengal tiger, but the arctic hare would fall dangerously short.

9 FEET
(2.75 M)

WINNER!

VS

6 FEET 9 INCHES **(2.1 M)**

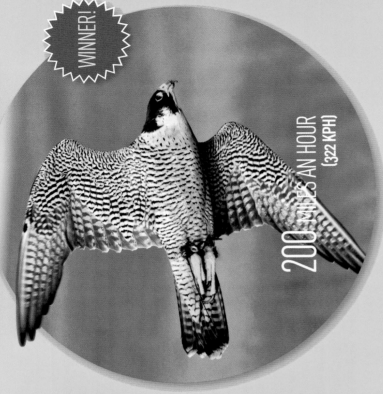

WINNER!

200 MILES AN HOUR
(322 KPH)

VS

13.5 MILES AN HOUR
(21.7 KPH)

SPEED DIVE!

The Chilean devil ray is probably the ocean's fastest diver, but it's no match for the peregrine falcon. This speed demon plummets 15 times faster through the air.

GLIDER

A dragon lizard could glide across the width of a football field, but the giant flying squirrel has been known to glide more than three times as far!

164 FEET
(50 M)

VS

525 FEET
(160 M)

WINNER!

THESE **DANCERS** **SKY-** PERFORM **HIGH** AWE-INSPIRING DANCE MOVES HUNDREDS OF FEET IN THE AIR.

BANDALOOP IS A PIONEERING GROUP OF **VERTICAL DANCERS.**

VERTICAL DANCERS PERFORM SUSPENDED FROM TALL STRUCTURES— **SKYSCRAPERS, BRIDGES,** AND **MOUNTAINS.**

SOME DANCERS ARE SKILLED **DEEP-SEA DIVERS** AND **SURFERS.** THEY HAVE NO FEAR OF **HEIGHTS.**

TRAINING IS INTENSE. IT COMBINES **DANCE TECHNIQUES** WITH **CLIMBING SKILLS** AND **YOGA.**

PERFORMERS USE THE SAME TYPES OF **CABLES** AND **HARNESSES** AS USED BY **ROCK CLIMBERS.**

FReAKY FLiERS
TAKE OFF!

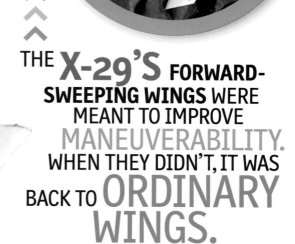

THE **X-29'S** **FORWARD-SWEEPING WINGS** WERE MEANT TO IMPROVE MANEUVERABILITY. WHEN THEY DIDN'T, IT WAS BACK TO **ORDINARY WINGS.**

THE **P-79W1** HYBRID AIRCRAFT CAN FLY **UNMANNED** AND **TOUCH DOWN ON WATER** USING AIR-CUSHIONED LANDING GEAR.

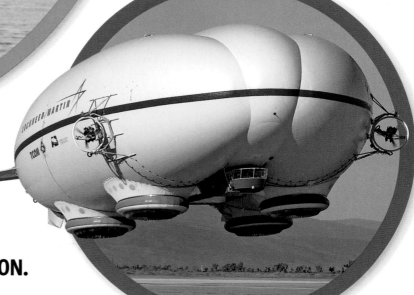

 THIS **VEGGIE-STYLE** AIRCRAFT JOINED OTHER HOMEMADE CONTRAPTIONS IN A RUSSIAN **FLYING-MACHINES COMPETITION.**

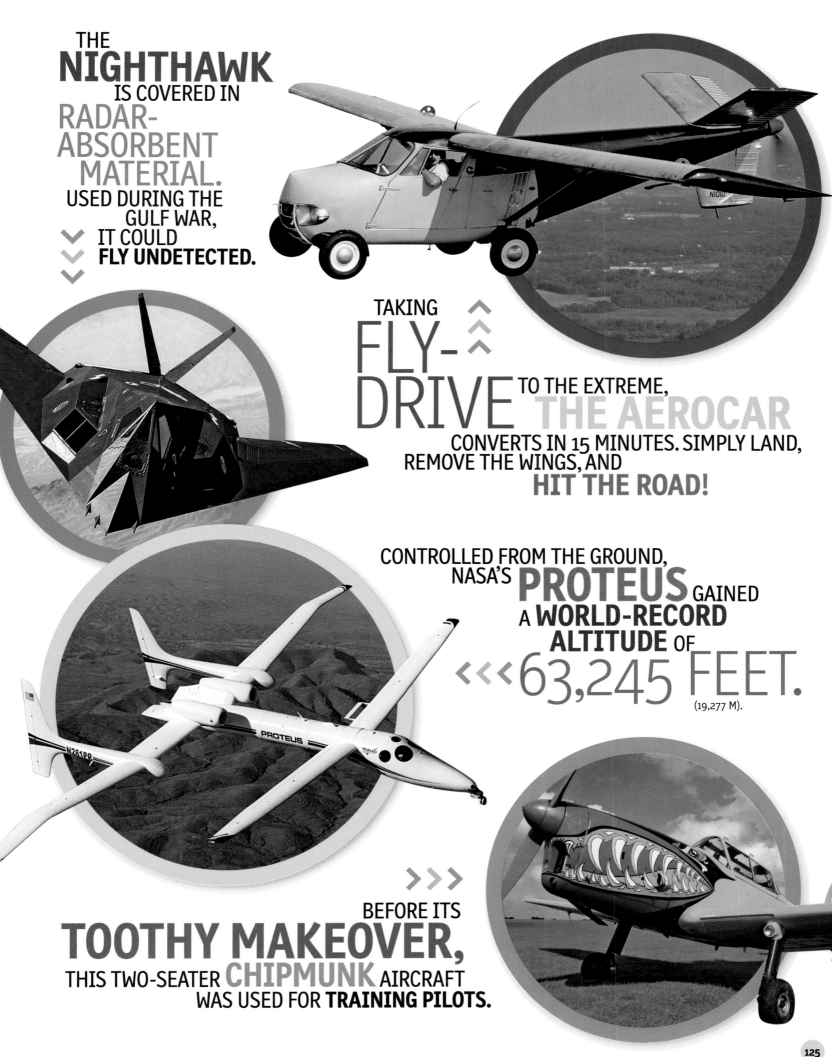

THE **NIGHTHAWK** IS COVERED IN **RADAR-ABSORBENT MATERIAL.** USED DURING THE GULF WAR, IT COULD **FLY UNDETECTED.**

TAKING **FLY-DRIVE** TO THE EXTREME, **THE AEROCAR** CONVERTS IN 15 MINUTES. SIMPLY LAND, REMOVE THE WINGS, AND **HIT THE ROAD!**

CONTROLLED FROM THE GROUND, NASA'S **PROTEUS** GAINED A **WORLD-RECORD ALTITUDE** OF <<< **63,245 FEET.** (19,277 M).

BEFORE ITS **TOOTHY MAKEOVER,** THIS TWO-SEATER **CHIPMUNK** AIRCRAFT WAS USED FOR **TRAINING PILOTS.**

In the 1700s, **French royalty** used **lace** instead of **toilet paper.**

This toilet-roll sculpture isn't the world's only toilet-inspired art. A Japanese novelist printed an entire book on toilet paper! See other potty-inspired stuff on page 142.

RIO RAMP DESIGN

#artecore

CHAPTER 7

ThAT'S GROSS!

EACH YEAR an adult sheds

8 POUNDS OF SKiN.

(3.6 kg)

Gather up all that dead skin and it would **WEIGH** as much as a **Siamese cat.**

ultimate secret revealed!

It's amazing that we have any skin left! In fact, our skin is made of layers, so we don't lose it all at once. Adults shed about one million skin cells every day from the top layer, the epidermis. But new cells continually replace dead cells. So what happens to the shed skin? It ends up everywhere—even in the dust you can see around you. Gross!

WHERE:
Manitoba, Canada

WHY IT'S AN INVASION:
The Narcisse Snake Pits provide a winter home for the world's **largest gathering** of red-sided garter snakes. A tunnel under a nearby highway allows the snakes to slither safely to the **dens.**

<<<

Ultimate iNVASiONS

WHERE:
Victoria, Australia

WHY IT'S AN INVASION:
Around **20,000 bees** cling to a clothesline. When bees swarm in spring, overcrowding forces the **queen** to leave the hive. She and her workers **cluster** wherever they can until a new home is found.

Bee-ware!

Raining Mayflies

WHERE:
Midwestern U.S.A.

WHY IT'S AN INVASION:
Mayflies emerge in large numbers in summer. In July 2014, so many were born in the Midwest that the weather radar picked them up as moderate **rain!**

Giant Jellies

WHERE:
Japan

WHY IT'S AN INVASION:
Since 2002, **millions** of gigantic jellyfish have collected in the seas around Japan. Some weigh as much as **450 pounds** (204 kg)—about the same as a **tiger.**

WHERE:
Colorado, U.S.A.

WHY IT'S AN INVASION:
Wet, warm weather brings **ladybugs** by the **millions.** Where they gather, they turn trees, plants, and even houses bright red.

Red Alert!

Greedy Grasshoppers

WHERE:
Florida, U.S.A.

WHY IT'S AN INVASION:
A handful of grasshoppers is harmless, but when they **breed** in large numbers they develop into **locusts** and swarm. Though rare, a swarm may contain **millions of insects** and can destroy crops.

9 STRANGE

THE **HUMAN NOSE** CAN **DISTINGUISH** ABOUT ONE TRILLION DIFFERENT ODORS.

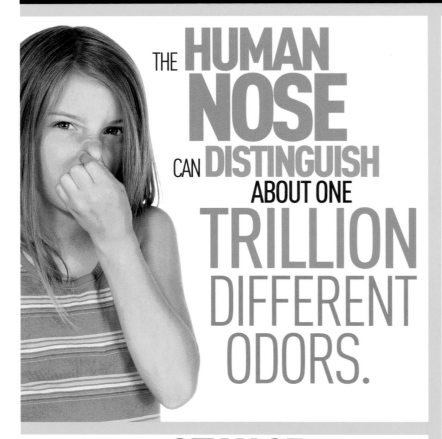

EVERYTHING SMELLS **HORRIBLE** TO PEOPLE WITH A CONDITION CALLED **CACOSMIA.** EVEN **FLOWERS** CAN SMELL LIKE **ROTTING FISH.**

IN 1858, THE SMELL OF **SEWAGE** IN **LONDON, ENGLAND,** WAS SO **BAD** THAT PEOPLE CALLED IT THE GREAT STINK.

SKUNKS PRODUCE SUCH A **POWERFUL ODOR** THAT PEOPLE CAN SMELL IT UP TO **1 MILE** (1.6 KM) **AWAY.**

FACTS ABOUT SMELL

THE **DURIAN FRUIT** IS **SO SMELLY** THAT IT'S BANNED ON SINGAPORE'S PUBLIC TRANSPORTATION.

THE **AFRICAN ELEPHANT** HAS **2,000 GENES** DEDICATED TO SMELLING—MORE THAN **ANY OTHER MAMMAL.**

The **DUNG BEETLE** pollinates a flower that smells like **POOP.**

PERSPIRATION IS **ODORLESS.** IT IS THE **BACTERIA** IN OUR **SWEAT** THAT CAUSE THE SMELL!

HUMANS CAN SMELL BEFORE THEY ARE BORN.

FISHY PEDICURE

Fast FACTS

NAME: The garra rufa fish, also called nibble or doctor fish

ORIGIN: Native to river basins in the Middle East

WHAT: Imported to the West to treat rough, dry feet

HOW: Dead skin is nibbled away, leaving healthy skin to thrive

WHEN: A spa in the United States introduced the treatment in 2008, attracting more than 6,000 people in the first five months

Is it SAFE?

Not everyone thinks the fishy footbath is a good thing. Several U.S. states and parts of Canada and Europe have banned the fish pedicure. Health regulators found that salons did not clean the fish tanks regularly. In addition, the same fish feed on different customers, and can spread infection from one person to another.

SOFT FEET COME AT A PRICE—UP TO $100 FOR ONE TREATMENT!

The tiny toothless **garra rufa fish** feasts on **DEAD SKIN!**

NOT JUST FOR PRETTY FEET! THE FISH PROVIDE RELIEF FROM SKIN DISORDERS SUCH AS PSORIASIS.

WILD GARRA RUFA FISH NIBBLE ON THE DEAD SCALES OF OTHER, LIVING FISH.

BEWARE IMPOSTERS! SOME SALONS USE CHIN CHIN FISH, WHOSE TEETH HAVE BEEN KNOWN TO DRAW BLOOD!

Poo Poo Platter

>>>

The bird-dropping spider folds itself into a pooplike blob that makes birds and wasps steer clear. When it's time for the spider's own dinner, it emits a scent that attracts the spider's favorite food—moths.

DON'T Eat That!

FROM SPIDERS THAT LOOK LIKE POOP

TO SMELLY BIRDS WITH **TOXIC FEATHERS**, THESE **CRAFTY CREATURES** AREN'T ON ANYONE'S MENU.

<<<

You've Been Warned

Look but don't touch the pitohui bird! It has lethal toxins in its wings and skin. If that wasn't enough, this New Guinea native gives off a strong, unpleasant smell to make itself even more unappetizing.

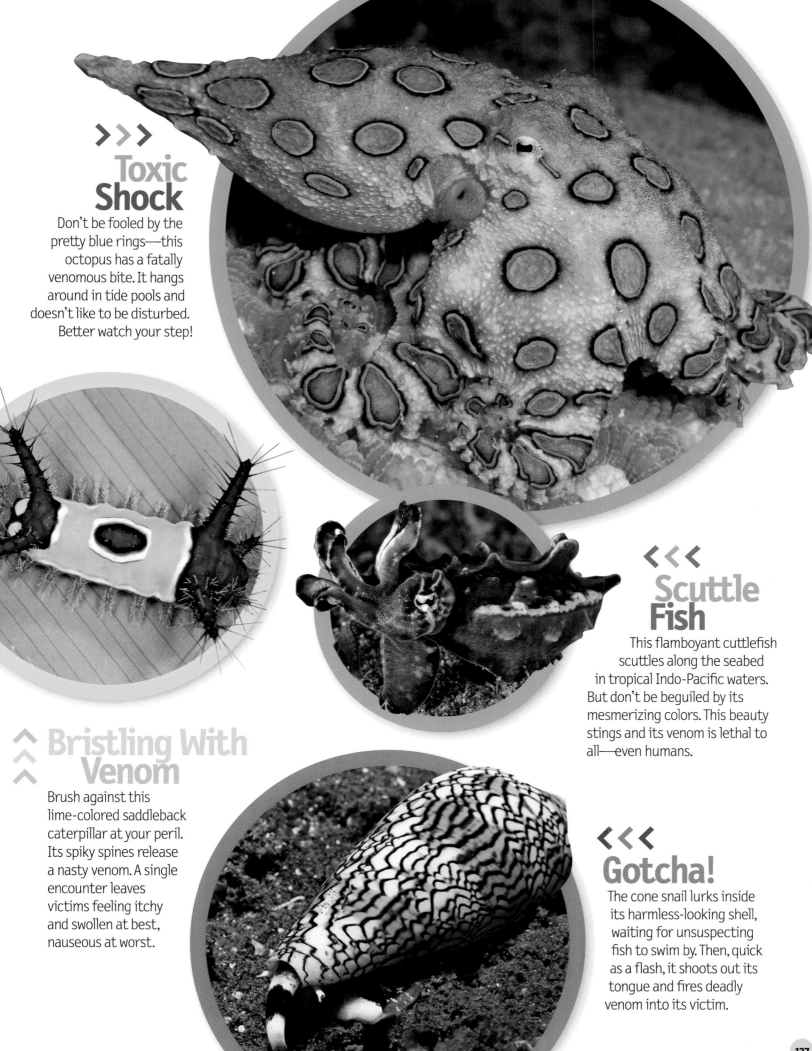

>>> Toxic **Shock**

Don't be fooled by the pretty blue rings—this octopus has a fatally venomous bite. It hangs around in tide pools and doesn't like to be disturbed. Better watch your step!

<<< Scuttle **Fish**

This flamboyant cuttlefish scuttles along the seabed in tropical Indo-Pacific waters. But don't be beguiled by its mesmerizing colors. This beauty stings and its venom is lethal to all—even humans.

^^^ Bristling With **Venom**

Brush against this lime-colored saddleback caterpillar at your peril. Its spiky spines release a nasty venom. A single encounter leaves victims feeling itchy and swollen at best, nauseous at worst.

<<< Gotcha!

The cone snail lurks inside its harmless-looking shell, waiting for unsuspecting fish to swim by. Then, quick as a flash, it shoots out its tongue and fires deadly venom into its victim.

<<<
Stinky Fish

WHERE:
Sweden

WHY IT'S GROSS:
The Surströmming Museum is dedicated to supersmelly **fermented herring.** The **Vikings** loved it, and it's still a **Swedish favorite.**

Disgusting Display

WHERE:
Meguro, Japan

WHY IT'S GROSS:
Where else would you find the world's **longest tapeworm** but at Japan's Parasitological Museum? This **29-foot** (8.8-m)- long specimen is one of 45,000 **parasites** in the collection.

>>>

Totally COOL GrOSS-Out museums

Creepy Mummies

WHERE:
Palermo, Sicily

WHY IT'S GROSS:
Nearly **8,000 mummies** greet visitors in the catacombs beneath Palermo's Capuchin monastery. The **oldest** is a preserved friar who **died in 1599.**

Smelly History

WHERE:
Paris, France

WHY IT'S GROSS:
Take a tour at the Sewer Museum to see waste passing along a stretch of Paris's 1,305-mile (2,100-km) sewage system.

WHERE:
San Antonio, Texas, U.S.A.

WHY IT'S GROSS:
Ex-plumber Barney Smith has a Toilet Seat Art Museum in his garage, with more than 1,000 exhibits. One even pays tribute to Michael Jackson.

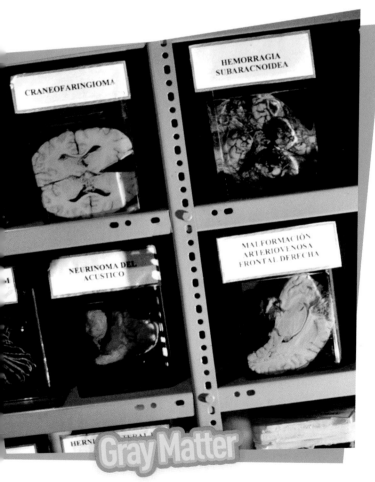

Gray Matter

WHERE:
Lima, Peru

WHY IT'S GROSS:
Behind the Institute of Neurological Science, the Brain Museum has some 3,000 brains on display.

Take a Seat!

ANCIENT EGYPTIANS GROUND DEAD MiCE INTO A PASTE FOR TREATING TOOTHACHES.

IN THE MIDDLE AGES, PEOPLE PASSED GAS INTO JARS AND TOOK SNIFFS TO WARD OFF PLAGUE.

IN THE 1600s SICK PEOPLE DRANK HEALTH-GIVING WATER THAT SMELLED LIKE ROTTEN EGGS IN BATH, ENGLAND.

ViCTORiAN DOCTORS ADVISED MEN TO GROW BEARDS TO PREVENT ILLNESS.

17TH-CENTURY HOME REMEDIES FOR BURNS INCLUDED GOOSE DUNG FRIED IN BUTTER.

IN THE FUTURE, GROUND-UP COCKROACH BRAINS COULD BE USED TO TREAT INFECTION.

A TRADITIONAL CHINESE RECIPE FOR SOOTHING SORE JOINTS INCLUDES SNAKE OIL.

RED, SLIMY HIPPO SWEAT CAN BE USED AS SUNSCREEN.

<<< **POTTY** ON **WHEELS!** MADE IN **INDIA**, THIS **FIVE-WHEELED CAR** CAN TRAVEL UP TO **30 MILES AN HOUR** (50 KPH).

TOTALLY AWESOME Toilets

<<< THIS **CAMERA-SHAPED** BUILDING IN **CHINA** IS REALLY A **RESTROOM.**

A **SKATEBOARDER ROLLS IN** ON A GIANT **SCULPTURE** >>> THAT IS PART OF AN **ARTS FESTIVAL** IN **RIO DE JANEIRO, BRAZIL.**

THIS **CHINESE SCULPTURE** FEATURES
<<< **10,000**
TOILETS, URINALS,
AND **SINKS,** ALL
FLUSHING TO MAKE
A WATERFALL.

KIDS >>>
SLIDE
INTO A
GIANT
TOILET
AT THIS
JAPANESE
MUSEUM EXHIBIT.

<<< WITH ITS **TOILET-SHAPED SEAT,** THIS
TOKYO **MOTORBIKE** USES FUEL MADE FROM
ANIMAL WASTE.

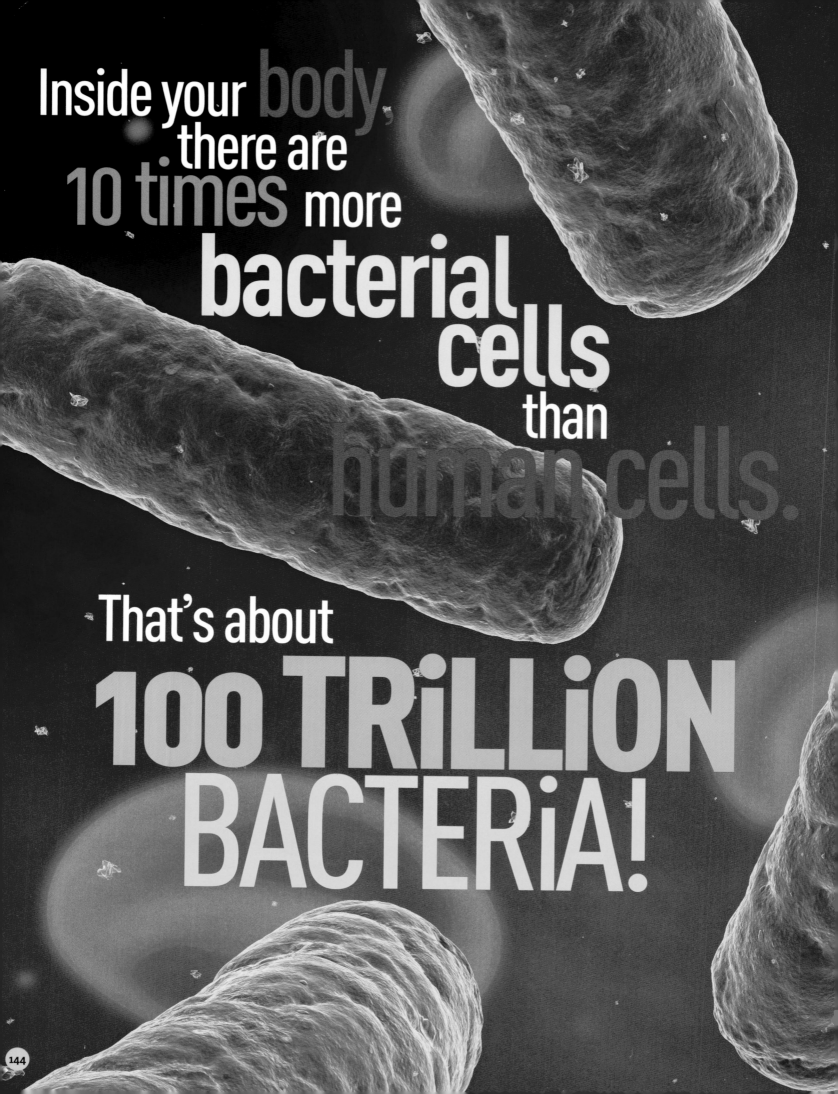

Inside your body, there are 10 times more bacterial cells than human cells.

That's about 100 TRiLLiON BACTERiA!

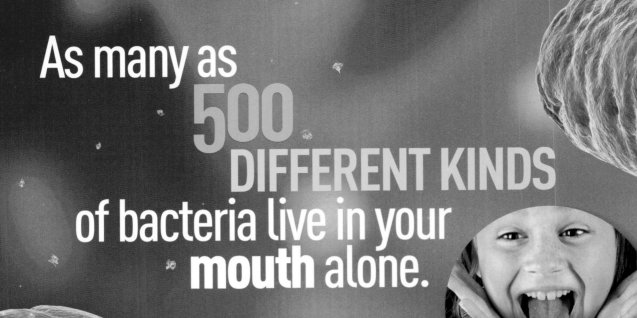

As many as 500 DIFFERENT KINDS of bacteria live in your **mouth** alone.

ultimate secret revealed!

Does this mean that we're mostly bacteria? Not exactly! Bacteria are microorganisms, so they are much smaller than human cells and take up only one to three percent of our body weight. Although they're tiny, many bacteria are disease-fighting, vitamin-making powerhouses. They break down food so our bodies can digest it. And they keep us healthy by teaching our bodies how to fight the bad bacteria that make us sick. We couldn't survive without them. So, don't freak out—bacteria can be friendly!

8

ReALLy WiLD!

Every spring, about 300 baby bats are rescued in Atherton, Australia. Sometimes, rescuers find a pup's mother and they are reunited! Read all about other rescued animals on page 166.

<<<
Home Alone

WHERE:
Secret World Wildlife Rescue, Somerset, England

WHY THEY'RE BUDDIES:
This **badger-otter** pair formed a unique bond after being rescued from the wild as **orphans**.

BEST BUDDiES

Check out these **oddball** animal friends.

WHERE:
Devon, England

⌄ WHY THEY'RE BUDDIES:
⌄ At feeding time on the farm, **springer spaniel**
⌄ Jess is on hand to help with orphaned **lambs**.

Playing Mom

Fast Friends

⌃ WHERE:
⌃ **Myrtle Beach Safari,**
⌃ **South Carolina, U.S.A.**

WHY THEY'RE BUDDIES:
Grizzly bear cub Bam Bam and his **chimp** playmate, Vali, love to have **fun**. When they grow up, Bam Bam will be **nine times** Vali's size!

Deer Friend

WHERE:
Secret World Wildlife Rescue, Somerset, England

WHY THEY'RE BUDDIES:
When frightened little **fawn** Cindy arrived at the rescue center, it was gentle giant Rocky, a **Great Dane**, who made her feel **safe.**

WHERE:
Busch Gardens, Tampa, Florida, U.S.A.

WHY THEY'RE BUDDIES:
A 3-year-old **giraffe** called Bea and Wilma, a 10-year-old **ostrich**, have 65 acres (26 ha) of safari park to roam and yet the two are almost **inseparable.**

Tall Story

Baby Love

WHERE:
Taman Safari Zoo, West Java, Indonesia

WHY THEY'RE BUDDIES:
When a mom rejected her **tiger cub,** zoologists paired it with an orphaned **orangutan.** The two baby animals love **hugs!**

CHoC-TASTiC!

Chocolate hits the catwalk with CLOTHES that look good enough to EAT!

THIS ELABORATE, CHOCOLATE, BIRD'S-NEST GOWN WAS DESIGNED BY JEAN-CLAUDE JEANSON. IT EVEN FEATURES LIVE BIRDS.

SOME DESIGNERS PAINT FABRIC WITH MELTED CHOCOLATE, ADDING CHOCOLATE TREATS AS EMBELLISHMENTS.

DESIGNS CAN TAKE ABOUT TWO WEEKS TO CREATE.

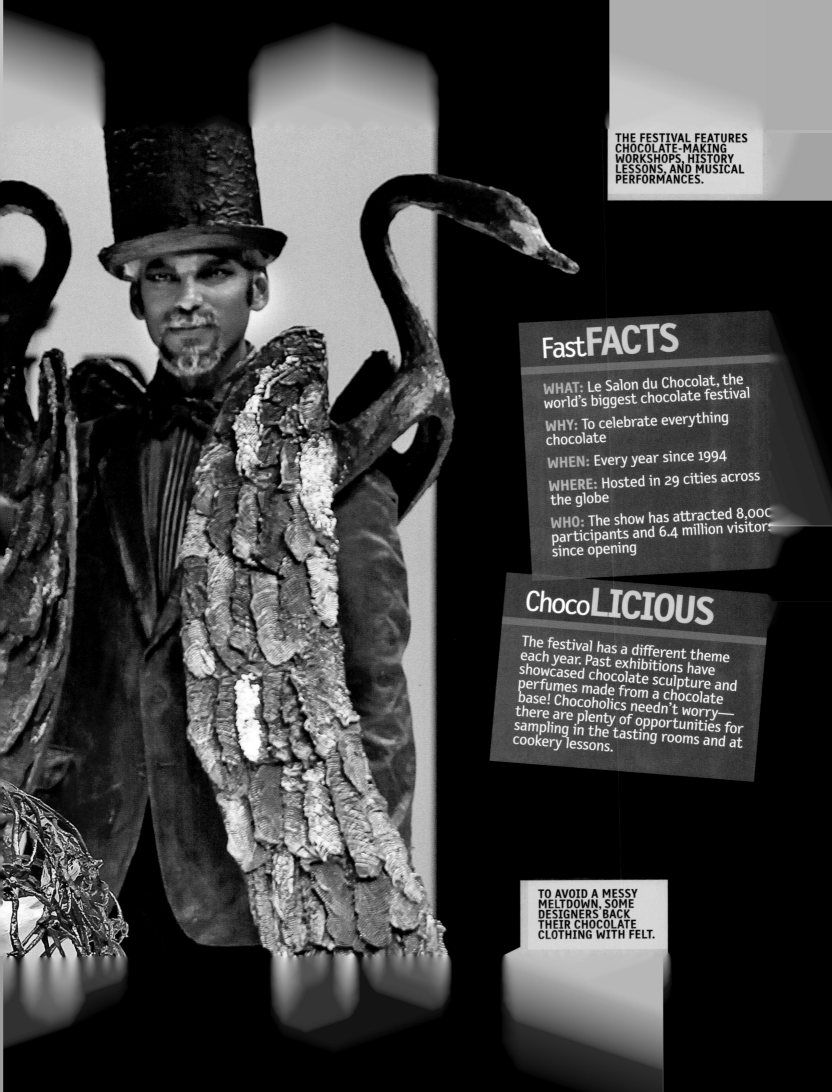

THE FESTIVAL FEATURES CHOCOLATE-MAKING WORKSHOPS, HISTORY LESSONS, AND MUSICAL PERFORMANCES.

Fast**FACTS**

WHAT: Le Salon du Chocolat, the world's biggest chocolate festival

WHY: To celebrate everything chocolate

WHEN: Every year since 1994

WHERE: Hosted in 29 cities across the globe

WHO: The show has attracted 8,000 participants and 6.4 million visitors since opening

Choco**LICIOUS**

The festival has a different theme each year. Past exhibitions have showcased chocolate sculpture and perfumes made from a chocolate base! Chocoholics needn't worry—there are plenty of opportunities for sampling in the tasting rooms and at cookery lessons.

TO AVOID A MESSY MELTDOWN, SOME DESIGNERS BACK THEIR CHOCOLATE CLOTHING WITH FELT.

WHAT IS IT?
Living Bridge

WHY IT'S CRAZY:
Hundreds of tiny fire **ants** lock their bodies together to bridge a gap in midair.

Teamwork!

<<<

Roll Up

WHAT IS IT?
Rolling Bridge, London, England

WHY IT'S CRAZY:
Powered by hydraulic cylinders, this 39-foot (12-m)-long footbridge curls up to let river traffic through.

CRAZY Crossings

>>>

Fiery Beast

WHAT IS IT?
Dragon Bridge, Da Nang, Vietnam

WHY IT'S CRAZY:
This 2,165-foot (660-m)-long monster bridge **breathes real fire** from its mouth.

WHAT IS IT?
Moses Bridge, Fort de Roovere, the Netherlands

WHY IT'S CRAZY:
Invisible from a distance, this bridge appears to **split the water**—like the **biblical story** of Moses parting the Red Sea.

Parting the Water

Tree Tunnel

WHAT IS IT?
Chandelier Tree, Leggett, California, U.S.A.

WHY IT'S CRAZY:
You can walk or drive right through this 315-foot (96-m)-tall **giant redwood tree.** It's more than **2,000 years old!**

Blooming Bridge

WHAT IS IT?
Wisteria Tunnel, Kawachi Fuji Gardens, Japan

WHY IT'S CRAZY:
The cascading **flowers** of 150 wisteria plants make a stunning tunnel from April to May. **Twenty species** make up the different colors.

In MOROCCO, GOATS

climb trees to get their favorite food.

→ The goats climb branches as high as **30 feet** (9 m) to eat the **argan tree's berries.**

→ As many as **16** goats might balance in an argan tree at once.

→ Goats' **hooves** have two toes that **grip** almost like fingers. Their feet have **soft soles,** which stop them from **slipping.**

→ Locals **grind** argan berries to produce an **oil** used in **cooking** and **cosmetics.** Sometimes these berries are sifted from goat **manure.**

→ The **argan tree** rarely grows taller than **30 feet** (10 m) and can live for up to **200** years.

ANIMAL Super-powers

THESE AWESOME
CREATURES HAVE **MIND-BLOWING TRICKS** UP THEIR SLEEVES!

Uncommon Sense

It may be funny looking, but the platypus has something most animals don't. When hunting underwater, it closes its eyes and ears and relies on electric sensors in its bill. The sensors pick up flickers of electricity from small animals, guiding the platypus straight to its dinner.

Flexible Fowl

There's no sneaking up on an owl! An owl has supersharp vision, but it can't move its eyes. Instead, it can swivel its head 270 degrees—almost all the way around! Most animals can't do this, but owls have specially adapted bones and blood vessels. Cool!

<<< Magnet Mouth

Ocean-dwelling chitons don't have brains, but they do have the strongest teeth in the world—and they're magnetic! When they wear out, new ones move forward to replace them. These mollusks use their strong chompers to scrape algae from rocks.

Slime Attack!

Don't let its looks fool you. The velvet worm is soft and small, but it has a secret weapon. It paralyzes prey with a fierce blast of slime from two tubes on its head. Gotcha!

>>>

<<<

Armed and Dangerous

Sharks have protective eyelids and skin that heals superfast. They have amazing hearing, too, and can smell a single drop of blood in one million drops of water.

<<<

Master Mimic

The superb lyrebird is a great copycat! This feathered show-off belts out sounds that mimic at least 20 different birds, including cockatoos and magpies. But the talent doesn't stop there. This Australian rain forest songbird also copies man-made sounds like chain saws and car alarms!

Lightning STRIKES the EIFFEL TOWER about 30 times a YEAR.

ultimate secret revealed!

Lightning can be five times hotter than the sun, so why doesn't the Eiffel Tower melt? Lightning often hits the tower because, at 1,062 feet (324 m) tall, it's the tallest structure in the area and is made of metal. Metals are good conductors (they allow electricity to pass through easily), which is why the Eiffel Tower has lightning rods fitted to its top. Since lightning always follows the easiest route to the ground, it strikes the lightning rods before hitting the tower. It then shoots down along metal cables, which carry the lightning's powerful electric charge deep into the ground. There, the surrounding earth is a poor conductor and makes the charge—and its heat—harmless!

A lightning **BOLT** contains enough **energy** to cook about **100,000** pieces of toast!

RED HAIR IS MORE COMMON IN SCOTLAND THAN ANYWHERE ELSE IN THE WORLD.

THE TINY COUNTRY OF LiECHTENSTEiN IS THE WORLD'S LARGEST PRODUCER OF FALSE TEETH AND SAUSAGE CASINGS.

NASA BUILT THE MAIN RUNWAY FOR **GAMBIA'S** AIRPORT AS AN EMERGENCY LANDING SPOT FOR THE **SPACE SHUTTLE.**

ANTIGUA HAS **365' BEACHES,** ONE FOR EACH DAY OF THE YEAR.

IN CHINA, POLICE USE **GEESE** TO HELP CATCH CRIMINALS.

ICELAND & THE FAROE iSLANDS ARE THE ONLY COUNTRIES IN THE WORLD WITHOUT **MOSQUiTOES.**

ISRAEL'S NATIONAL PARKS MAKE UP **1/5** OF THE **COUNTRY.**

210 DAYS LONG.

ACCORDING TO THE BALINESE CALENDAR, ONE YEAR IS

IN **1990,** NEW ZEALAND'S GOVERNMENT APPOINTED A NATIONAL **WiZARD.**

10 FASCINATING

JOHN QUINCY ADAMS HAD A **PET ALLiGATOR.**

RUTHERFORD B. HAYES OWNED THE **FiRST SiAMESE** CAT iN AMERiCA.

GEORGE WASHINGTON'S **HORSES** HAD THEIR **TEETH** BRUSHED EVERY MORNiNG.

WOODROW WILSON KEPT A HERD of **SHEEP** ON THE **WHITE HOUSE** LAWN DURING WORLD WAR I.

ABRAHAM LINCOLN GAVE HIS CHILDREN'S **PET turkey** A PRESIDENTIAL **PARDON** FOR THANKSGIVING.

PRESiDENTiAL PETS

HERBERT HOOVER'S more unusual pets included an **OPOSSUM.**

GEORGE W. BUSH'S DOG **SPOTTY** WAS THE ONLY DOG TO LIVE AT THE **WHITE HOUSE** UNDER TWO PRESIDENTS.

ULYSSES S. GRANT was the **only** **PRESiDENT** TO GET A *SPEEDING TICKET* WHILE iN OFFICE—HE was riding his *HORSE!*

EXPLORERS **LEWIS** AND **CLARK** GAVE **THOMAS JEFFERSON** **2 GRIZZLY BEAR CUBS.**

THE **OBAMAS** KEEP BEES— THEY HAVE **70,000!**

70,000 plants

make up this giant **living sculpture** in Montreal, Canada.

→ This **49-foot** (15-m) -tall sculpture—called **Mother Earth**—is an exhibit at the International Mosaiculture Competition, a celebration of **gardening** and **horticulture.**

→ **Mosaïculture** is a French word used to describe **3-D sculptures** made from many colorful **plants.**

→ The specialty sculptors created, designed, and built this sculpture's basic **metal form,** topped it with a **steel mesh,** then planted it with **flowers.**

→ Mother Earth's **skin** is santolina, an evergreen shrub; petunias and ipomeas make up her **hair.**

→ The **water** cascading from Mother Earth's palm falls **13 feet** (4 m) to the pool below.

Caring for Koalas

^^^ **WHERE IS IT?**
Port Macquarie, Australia

^^ **WHY IT'S WILD:**
Rescuers from the Koala Hospital find koalas that need help and take them to the hospital. They stay until they're **happy and healthy.**

Unusually WILD Hospitals

^^^ **Help for Hedgehogs**

^^ **WHERE IS IT?**
Haddenham, England

WHY IT'S WILD:
Badgers, otters, hedgehogs, and other English **wildlife** get star **treatment** at **St. Tiggywinkles** Hospital.

Baby Elephant Rescue

WHERE IS IT?
Nairobi, Kenya

WHY IT'S WILD:
The **Orphans' Project,** part of the David Sheldrick Wildlife Trust, saves baby **elephants and rhinos** who are all alone in the wild.

<<<

Treatment for Turtles

WHERE IS IT?
Marathon, Florida, U.S.A.

WHY IT'S WILD:
The Turtle Hospital has helped over **1,500 sick sea turtles** so far! When they get better, staff release them **into the wild.**

<<<

Going Batty

WHERE IS IT?
Atherton, Australia

WHY IT'S WILD:
Tolga Bat Hospital puts **orphan bats** near wild bat mothers and babies. The **mothers teach** the orphans all the bat basics!

Bonobo Babysitter

WHERE IS IT?
Near Kinshasa, Democratic Republic of the Congo

WHY IT'S WILD:
Lola Ya Bonobo, which means "paradise for bonobos," is the world's **only sanctuary** for orphaned bonobos. How **cool** is that?

Saving Sloths

Penshurt, Costa Rica

WHY IT'S WILD:
The **Sloth Sanctuary** has rescued over **500 sloths** since 1992, many of them orphans.

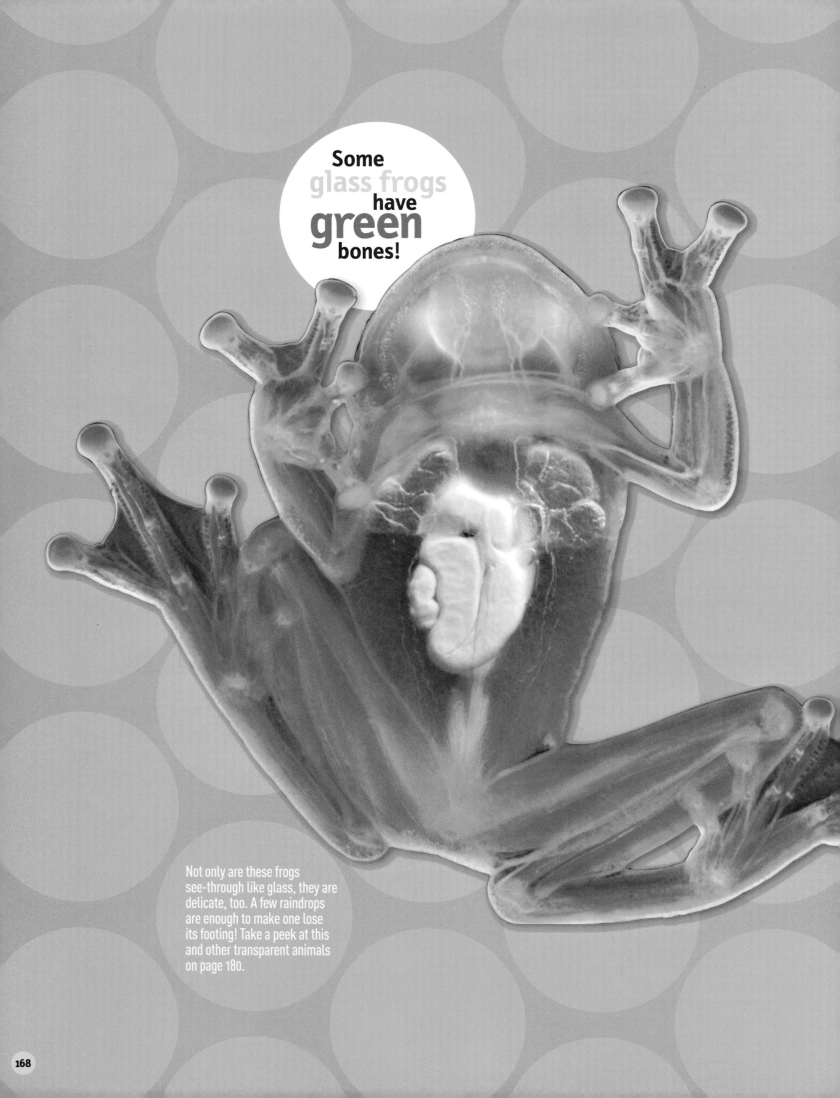

Some **glass frogs** have **green** bones!

Not only are these frogs see-through like glass, they are delicate, too. A few raindrops are enough to make one lose its footing! Take a peek at this and other transparent animals on page 180.

Eye-
PoPPeRS

Big Bangs!

THE **FIRST FIRECRACKERS** were **BAMBOO SHOOTS** stuffed with **SULFUR**, **CHARCOAL**, and **POTASSIUM**.

THE **CHINESE** INVENTED FIREWORKS **2,000 YEARS** AGO AND THEY'VE BEEN LIGHTING UP THE NIGHT **EVER SINCE!**

90 PERCENT of **ALL FIREWORKS** still come from **CHINA**.

DISNEY WORLD, Florida, U.S.A., holds **MORE** than **1,000** fireworks **SHOWS** a **YEAR.**

The **LARGEST** fireworks **SPECTACLE** was in **DUBAI**. It consisted of **479,651** fireworks.

A firework that **MISFIRES** and **EXPLODES** within the **LAUNCH TUBE** is called a **"FLOWERPOT."**

1.6 MILLION people attend the **NEW YEAR'S EVE** display at Australia's **SYDNEY OPERA HOUSE.**

SPARKLERS can BURN as hot as 1,200 °F (648.9°C). GLASS MELTS at 900 °F (482°C)!

ALUMINUM and IRON flakes create SPARKLES; TITANIUM powder makes a loud BLAST.

Different ELEMENTS make up the COLORS— COBALT for BLUE, TITANIUM and MAGNESIUM for SILVER or WHITE.

The SHAPE of a fireworks EXPLOSION depends on HOW the basic FUEL and COLOR PELLETS are PACKED.

Razor Sharp

A barber in Texas, U.S.A., gives fans the **buzz cut** of their dreams. Using a traditional razor, scissors, and eyeliner pencils, the master clipper transforms the **backs of heads** into famous faces, from **Steve Jobs** to Albert Einstein.

WACKY and WILD art

Double Take

Masterpieces of **culinary art,** these tomatoes are made of sweet almond **marzipan.** Eat them for dessert, not on your salad!

These **imitations** look so real you won't **believe** your **eyes.**

Handy Snake!

Don't be surprised if this **slithery snake** wants to shake your hand. It's really one of artist Guido Daniele's super-realistic "handimals."

What a way to make an entrance! Kurt Wenner's amazing **3-D street art** makes this new **car launch** in South Africa one to remember.

Watch Out!
>>>

Sweet Meat
^
^ **Cranberry sauce** isn't on the menu with this "turkey." Try **ice cream**—it's a yummy **cake!**
^

Heads Up!

Look closely—even the rabbit wants a bite >>> of this **tasty picnic!** An Israeli **hat designer** creates mini-meals to perch on your head.

BORN DIFFERENT

These wild **babies** look nothing like their parents!

BABY CAMOUFLAGE

WHO'S THE BABY? Malayan tapir

SPOT THE DIFFERENCE:
Baby tapirs are born with striped, spotted fur—perfect camouflage for the dappled light of their forest habitat. By six months, this calf will look just like its mom, with thick, black-and-white fur.

OCEAN HEAVYWEIGHT

WHO'S THE BABY? Ocean sunfish

SPOT THE DIFFERENCE:
The ocean sunfish measures 0.04 inches (1 mm) when born, and has a tail and spikes that disappear as it grows bigger. An adult sunfish can weigh a whopping 5,000 pounds (2,268 kg)!

ROYAL FAMILY

WHO'S THE BABY? King penguin

SPOT THE DIFFERENCE:
These baby penguins look so different from their parents that scientists once thought they were a completely different species! At about a year, the fluffy brown feathers molt and the penguins get cool orange markings and a waterproof coat just like Mom and Dad!

WHAT A HONKER!

WHO'S THE BABY?
Proboscis monkey

SPOT THE DIFFERENCE:
Proboscis monkeys are born with black fur that turns orange by four months. Within a year, the nose starts to grow. Female monkeys have smaller noses, but if he's a boy, this little monkey will end up with a supersize honker, just like his dad.

FEAR OF THE COLOR BLUE IS CALLED **CYANOPHOBiA.**

ACCORDING TO STUDIES, PEOPLE THINK **HOT CHOCOLATE** TASTES **BETTER** IN AN ORANGE MUG.

THE **AZTEC** VALUED **RED DYE** **MORE** THAN GOLD.

SHEPHERDS BELiEVED **ONE BLACK SHEEP** iN A FLOCK BROUGHT **GOOD LUCK.**

THERE ARE **GREEN BIRDS, REPTILES, FISH, AND INSECTS**—BUT NO GREEN MAMMALS.

IN 1542 THE WORD ORANGE WAS FIRST USED TO NAME THE COLOR. BEFORE THAT, IT ONLY NAMED THE FRUIT.

JUST AS HUMAN BLOOD IS RED WHEN OXYGENATED, A LOBSTER'S BLOOD IS BLUE.

PURPLE DYE IN ANCIENT ROME, TYRIAN WAS WORTH MORE THAN GOLD.

THE GARFISH HAS GREEN BONES.

An **EAGLE** can spot **prey** from up to **2miles** (3 km) away— that's **5 TIMES** as far as a **HUMAN** can see.

A **fly's-eye** view is all in
slow motion,
meaning it can register what it sees—and
react to it—much faster
than a
human.

**ultimate
secret
revealed!**

What do animals really see? The world looks quite different to many animals, depending on the kind of eyes they have. Bees and other insects can see ultraviolet (UV) light, which is invisible to the human eye. This UV vision leads them straight to the nectar in flowers—crucial if you happen to be a bee. Meanwhile, seeing at night is no problem for bush babies. Their huge eyes let in extra light so they can spot tiny insects to eat. Horses have a blind spot when they look straight ahead, but having eyes on the sides of their heads gives them almost 360-degree vision. How cool is that?

See-through Creatures

FROM DEEP-SEA DWELLERS TO COLOR-CHANGING BEETLES IN OUR OWN BACKYARDS, THESE ANIMALS ARE CLEARLY EXTRAORDINARY!

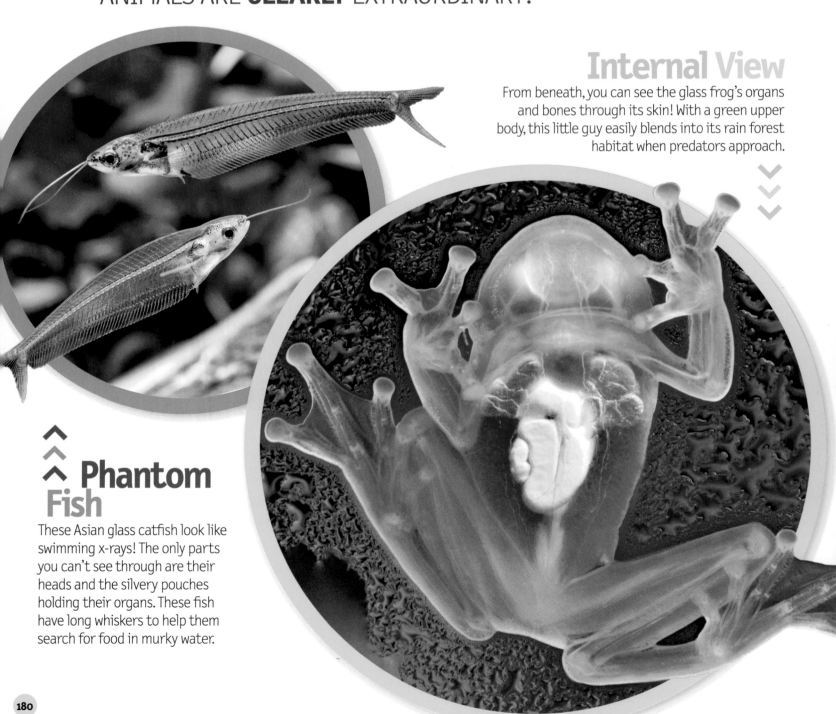

Internal View

From beneath, you can see the glass frog's organs and bones through its skin! With a green upper body, this little guy easily blends into its rain forest habitat when predators approach.

Phantom Fish

These Asian glass catfish look like swimming x-rays! The only parts you can't see through are their heads and the silvery pouches holding their organs. These fish have long whiskers to help them search for food in murky water.

Steer Clear!

The shell of this golden tortoise beetle changes from red and black to gold to scare off predators. The edges of its shell are flattened and clear, making it difficult for would-be attackers to see how to grasp its body.

>>>

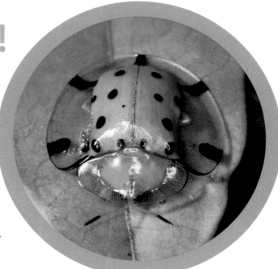

^
^
^
Ocean Ghost

At 18 inches (45 cm) long, the glass octopus has a transparent body—perfect for hiding from enemies in deep ocean water. Seen under light, its suckers look like strings of glowing beads.

>>>

Stained Glass

Unlike other butterflies, the stunning glasswing butterfly does not have colored scales on its wings—only the outer edges have some tint. This clever camouflage makes this delicate beauty almost invisible to birds.

<<<

Crystal Clear

This glassy little shrimp is busy in its underwater world. It hides among sea anemones and gets to work cleaning parasites from passing fish. The fish are happy clients, and don't eat the shrimp. It's a win-win!

ON THE **OTHER SIDE** IS A PORTRAIT OF SHOWMAN **BUFFALO BILL CODY.**

ARTIST JOHN LOPEZ MADE THIS LIFE-SIZE BUFFALO OUT OF SCRAP METAL.

LOPEZ'S OTHER LARGE-SCALE SCULPTURES INCLUDE A **TEXAS LONGHORN,** A **GRIZZLY BEAR,** AND A *TRICERATOPS.*

JUMPING SPIDERS

are not just LONG-JUMP CHAMPS, they also have the best

vision

of any spider.

→ What makes these little guys see so well? Two **principal eyes**—tubes that run into a jumping spider's head—gauge **depth.** Four **additional eyes** on the top of the spider's head sense **motion.**

→ The jumping spider can leap up to **50 times** its own body length.

→ These fierce hunters are **tiny!** Even the biggest is only about **0.5 inches** (1.3 cm) long.

→ There are **5,000** types of jumping spiders and they live all over the world—even on **Mount Everest!**

→ **Opposites attract!** Male jumping spiders put on a **dance show** to attract females.

fact finder

CHINESE **SAILORS** HAD
CHINESE CRESTED DOGS
ON BOARD SHIP, BECAUSE THEY
WERE GOOD AT CATCHING RATS.

BEFORE
1920, COTTON CANDY
WAS CALLED
FAIRY FLOSS.

FLYBOARDERS PERFORM THE **CORKSCREW** BY DIVING **BACKWARD** AND **TWISTING** THE HOSE.

THE CANADIAN-MADE **CHIPMUNK** WAS FOLLOWED BY **AIRPLANES** CALLED THE **BEAVER** AND THE **OTTER.**

fact finder

A **TREEHOPPER'S POOP** IS CALLED **HONEYDEW**, BECAUSE IT IS SO **SWEET**. ANTS LOVE TO **EAT IT!**

credits

COVER AND FRONT MATTER

Cover: (UPLE), Geoffrey Robinson/Rex/Rex USA; (UP CTR), Panthera/Alamy; (UPRT), James D. Morgan/Rex/REX USA; (CTR RT), Rolf NussbaumerPhotography/Alamy; (LOLE), Richard Austin/Rex/Rex USA; (LOCTR), SWNS/Splash News/Newscom; (UP LE), James D. Morgan/Rex/REX USA; (LO LE), Panthera/Alamy; (LOLE), Richard Austin/Rex USA; (CTR), Rolf Nussbaumer Photography/Alamy; Spine: Kyodo/Newscom; Back cover: (UP), Franco Tempesta/National Geographic; (CTR RT), Justin Lewis/Getty Images; 2-3, Christian Pondella/Red Bull/SIPA/Newscom; 4 (UP RT), Ben Russell/www.socialeyesphoto.com; (LO LE), Danita Delimont/Alamy; 5 (LO LE), China Daily/Reuters/Corbis; (CTR RT), Suzi Eszterhas/Minden Pictures/FLPA

CHAPTER 1

6-7, Wong Campion/Reuters/Corbis; 8-9, Chris Helgren/Reuters/Corbis; 8 (CTR LE), Franziska Kraufmann/EPA/Newscom; (LO RT), Wong Campion/Reuters/Corbis; 9 (UP LE), Ben Russell/www.socialeyesphoto.com; (LO RT), Charles McQuillan/Getty Images; (CTR RT), Markku Ojala/epa/Corbis; 10-11, Galen Rowell/Corbis; 11 (LO RT), David Acosta Allely/123rf; 12-13, John Devries/Science Source; 12 (LO RT), Shutterstock/Jiang Hongyan; (LO RT), Shutterstock/Photo Melon; 13 (CTR RT), Shutterstock/sunabesyou; (LO RT), Shutterstock/images.etc; (LO LE), Shutterstock/Ljupco Smokovski; 14 (UP), Jeremy Woodhouse/Getty Images; (LO RT), Izf/Shutterstock; (LO LE), David Steele/Shutterstock; 15 (UP LE), Gunther Marx Photography/Corbis; (LO), Igor Sasin/AFP/Getty Images; (UP RT), muratart/Shutterstock; 16-17, Stephen Dalton/Nature Picture Library; 18 (UP LE), Sandesh Kadur/Nature Picture Library; (CTR), Norbert Wu/Science Faction/Corbis; (LO LE), Mitsuhiko Imamori/Minden Pictures/FLPA; 19 (UP LE), Getty Images/Michael & Patricia Fogden; (UP RT), Bork/Shutterstock; (LO), Simon G/Shutterstock; 20-21, Balazs Mohai/epa/Corbis; 22 (UP RT), Shutterstock/svry; (CTR), Shutterstock/Gtranquillity; (CTR RT), Shutterstock/LoloStock; (CTR), Shutterstock/Chokniti Khongchum; (LO), Shutterstock/Africa Studio; 23 (LO RT), Getty Images/Design Pics RF/Ron Nickel; (UP RT), Shutterstock/Hurst Photo; 23 (CTR RT), Shutterstock/Picsfive; (CTR LE), MSPhotographic/Shutterstock; 24-25, Enahm Hof/Barcroft USA/Barcoft Media/Getty Images

CHAPTER 2

26, Kyodo/Newscom; 28-29, Betty Chu/Splash News/Corbis; 30 (UP), James D. Morgan/Rex/REX USA; (UP LE), Tony Margiocchi; (LO LE), Alan Diaz/AP Photo; 31 (UP RT), Julien Warnand/epa/Corbis; (CTR), Kena Betancur/Getty Images; (LO RT), Christopher Cutro/Miami Dade Fair and Expo; 32-33, Imaginechina/Rex; 34 (UP LE), SCIEPRO/Getty Images; (UP RT), Shutterstock/Igor Karasi; (LO RT), Shutterstock/Ferenc Szelepcsenyi; (LO LE), Jan Hamrsky/Nature Picture Library; 35 (LO LE), Geordie Torr/Alamy; (LO RT), Shutterstock/Hurst Photo; (UP RT), Shutterstock/Sailorr; (UP LE), Juniors Tierbildarchiv/Photoshot; 36-37, Weerakarn Satitniramai/Getty Images; 38 (UP LE), Steve Meddle/Rex/REX USA; (LO LE), Shutterstock/Africa Studio; (CTR RT), Kyodo/Newscom; 39 (CTR RT), Bruno Morandi/Robert Harding/Rex; (CTR LE), Heritage Images/Getty Images; (LO RT), Shutterstock/Eric Isselee; 40-41, MJT/AdMedia/Corbis; 42 (UP RT), David Wall/Alamy; (LO), Exotica/Alamy; (UP LE), Getty Images/kickstand; 43 (LO LE), Daniel Frauchiger; (UP), Photoshot/Bruce Adams/eye ubiquitous; (LO RT), Ritu Jethani/123rf; 44-45 (UP CTR), Ben Osborne/naturepl.com/NaturePL; (CTR), Shutterstock/Dynamicfoto; (CTR CTR), Shutterstock/Julia Remezova; (LO CTR), Shutterstock/Davydenko Yuliia; 45 (CTR RT), Shutterstock/Taina Sohlman

CHAPTER 3

46-47, ChinaFotoPress/Getty Images; 48-49, Courtesy AllRights-Reserved/Paulo Grangeon; 50 (LO LE), Studio 101/Alamy; (UP RT), Shutterstock/fivepointsix; (UP LE), Shutterstock/coprid; 51 (LO RT), Shutterstock/STILLFX; (UP RT), Shutterstock/David Crockett; (LO RT), Shutterstock/Alex James Bramwell; (UP RT), Shutterstock/Fabio Berti; (LO LE), Shutterstock/Nata789; (CTR LE), Shutterstock/Jagodka; 52-53, Shutterstock/Alexander A.Trofimov; 54 (UP RT), Shutterstock/Richard Peterson; (LO RT), Shutterstock/ArtFamily; 54-55, Shutterstock/Walter Quirtmair; 55 (CTR RT), Shutterstock/MO_SES Premium; (LO LE), Shutterstock/Julie Clopper; 56 (CTR LE), ilovedogs.com/Solent News/Rex/RE; (UP RT), customised by crystalrocked.com; (LO RT), The House of Solid Gold; 57 (UP LE), Xinhua News Agency/REX; (CTR RT), Gilbert Carrasquillo/FilmMagic/Getty; (CTR LE), Colin Bridges/Krispy Kreme; (UP LE), Shimansky; 58-59, Shutterstock/Triff; 58 (CTR LE), Shutterstock/Alan Uster; 59 (CTR RT), Shutterstock/Vibe Images; 60 (CTR RT), Shutterstock/Arena Photo UK; (UP LE), Shutterstock/Zerbor; (LO LE), Shutterstock/sukiyaki; 61 (UP RT), Shutterstock/DioGen; (CTR LE), Shutterstock/picturepartners; (LO RT), Shutterstock/redpip1984; 62-63, Karen Kasmauski/Corbis; 64 (LO), Shutterstock/Hurst Photo; 65 (UP), Shutterstock/Kellis; (CTR), Shutterstock/Quaoar

CHAPTER 4

66-67, Franck Fotos/Alamy; 68-69, James Morris; 70 (UP LE), Danita Delimont/Alamy; (UP LE), Getty Images/Moment Open/Yuko Yamada; (CTR RT), Barrett & MacKay/All Canada Photos/Photoshot; 71 (LO RT), Radius Images/Alamy; (LO LE), Franck Fotos/Alamy; (UP RT), T.C. Bird; 72-73, Solvin Zankl/Visuals Unlimited/Corbis; 74 (UP LE), Eric Baccega/Nature Picture Library/Corbis; (LO LE), Finca Bellavista/James Lozeau; (LO RT), Redwoods Treehouse; 75 (LO), Christian Kober/Getty Images; (UP LE), Peter Lundstrom WDO/www.treehotel.se; (CTR RT), David R. Gluns; 76-77, National Geographic; 78-79 (LO), Rodrusoleg/iStock; 78 (UP LE), Michael Urban/AFP/Getty Images; (UP RT), messenjah/iStock; (LO LE), AdShooter/Shutterstock; (LO RT), Mike Mergen/Bloomberg News/Getty Images; 79 (LO RT), The LIFE Images Collection/Getty; (UP LE), Jose Luis Pelaez/Getty Images; 80 (LO LE), All Canada Photos/Alamy; (UP LE), Bob Gomel/The LIFE Picture Collection/Getty; (LO RT), Shutterstock/bumihills; 81 (UP RT), Keith Levit/Design Pics/Getty; (LO LE), Shutterstock/T photography; (CTR RT), Ruth Hallam/123rf; 82-83, Mitsuaki Iwago/Minden Pictures; 84 (UP RT), Christopher Smith/AP Photo; (UP LE), Snap Stills/Rex/REX USA; (LO), Heidi Geraci/ThePictureEscape.com; 85 (UP RT), Clearwater Marine Aquarium; (CTR LE), Paul Drinkwater/NBC/NBCU Photo Bank via Getty Images; (LO RT), Durham/Oregon Zoo/Splash/Splash News/Corbis

CHAPTER 5

86, Photo by Rex/REX USA; 88-89, Shutterstock/CLIPAREA l Custom media; 89 (LO LE), Shutterstock/Maxim Blinkov; 90-91 (UP), Geoffrey Robinson/Rex/REX USA; 90 (LO LE), Photo by Rex/REX USA; (LO RT), WENN Ltd/Alamy; 91 (CTR RT), Solent News/Splash News/Newscom; (LO LE), Everett Kennedy Brown/epa/Corbis; 92-93, Ingo Arndt/naturepl.com/NaturePL; 94 (CTR LE), Phototake, Inc./Alamy; (UP LE), Shutterstock/Maksym Darakchi; (LO), Shutterstock/David Herraez Calzada; (UP RT), Shutterstock/Frank Rohde; (LO LE), Shutterstock/Ollyy; 95 (UP RT), Shutterstock/Sofiaworld; (CTR RT), Shutterstock/Iakov Kalinin; (LO), Shutterstock/Hermin; 96-97, Science Picture Co/Science Source; 96 (UP LE), Shutterstock/Neveshkin Nikolay; 97 (LO RT), Cgtoobox/Dreamstime; 98-99, Shutterstock/Repina Valeriya; 100 (LO LE), Tony Kyriacou/Rex/REX USA; (UP), WENN Ltd/Alamy; (LO RT), Junior D. Kannah/AFP/Getty Images; 101 (UP), Paul Darrow/Reuters/Corbis; (CTR LE), Toru Hanai/Reuters/Corbis; (LO RT), Yoshikazu Tsuno/AFP/Getty Images; 102-103, Getty Images/Science Faction/NASA; 103 (LO LE), Shutterstock/Maxx-Studio; (LO CTR), Shutterstock/Vlad_Nikon; 104 (UP LE), Shutterstock/Peter Zijlstra; (UP RT), Shutterstock/Phumphao Sumrankong; (LO LE), Shutterstock/Rita Kochmarjova; (LO RT), Michal Adamczyk; 105 (UP LE), Nico Smit/123rf; (UP RT), Eric Isselee/123rf; (LO RT), Dmitry Pistrov/123rf; (LO LE), Duncan Noakes/123rf

CHAPTER 6

106-107, David McHugh/Rex/REX USA; 109, Justin Lewis/Getty Images; 110 (LO LE), Alexander Korner/Action Press/Newscom; (UP LE), Andrea De Silva/Reuters/Corbis; (CTR LE), Albanpix Ltd/Rex/REX USA; 111 (UP RT), Splash News/Evento; (CTR RT), Daniel Roland/AP Photo; (LO LE), Garry Jones/AP Photo; 112-113 (BACK), Shutterstock/Rich Carey;112 (LO RT), Francois Xavier Marit/AFP/Getty Images; (UP LE), Shutterstock/Gunnar Pippel; 113 (UP), Alastair Pollock Photography/Getty Images/Flickr RF; (UP LE), Shutterstock/Andrea Izzotti; (CTR RT), Simone Gatterwe/123rf ; 114 (LO LE), Bettmann/Corbis; (UP), Alistair Berg/Getty Images; (L), Shutterstock/Lisa F. Young; (CTR RT), Shutterstock/AMA; 115 (LO CTR), General Photographic Agency/Getty Images; (CTR RT), Shutterstock/Dick Stada; 116-117, Shutterstock/iofoto; 118 (LO), SWNS/Splash News/Newscom; (UP RT), Xinhua/Zheng Peng/Newscom; (UP LE), Daphne Shapiro/The Plaza North Shopping Center; 119 (UP RT), David McHugh/Rex/REX USA; (LO), China Daily/Reuters; (UP LE), Judy Bellah/Getty Images/Lonely Planet Images; 120 (LO RT), Michael Durham/Minden Pictures/FLPA; (UP LE), Elena Duvernay/iStock; (UP RT), Shutterstock/Cheryl Ann Quigley; (LO LE), Matthias Breiter/Minden Pictures/FLPA; 121 (LO LE), Will Burrard-Lucas/NaturePL; (LO RT), Photo Researchers/FLPA; (UP LE), Reinhard Dirscherl/Oceans-Image/Photoshot; (UP RT), Steve Oehlenschlager/123rf; 122-123, Jerry Naunheim Jr.; 124, Nickolay Vinokurov/Demotix/Corbis; (UP LE), Getty Images/Science Faction; (LO RT), Lockhed Martin/Bob Driver; 125 (UP RT), Bruce Bisping/ZUMA Press/Corbis; (LO RT), Chris Mattison/Alamy; (CTR LE), age fotostock/Alamy; (LO LE), Tom Tschida/NASA; Dryden Flight Research Center

CHAPTER 7

126-127, Yasuyoshi Chiba/AFP/Getty Images; 128-129, Andrew Syred/Science Source; 129 (LO CTR), Shutterstock/DenisNata; (CTR RT), Shutterstock/Jagodka; 130 (LO RT), Laszlo Balogh/Reuters/Corbis; (LO LE), Brian Gardiner/Solent News/Rex USA; (UP LE), Norbert Rosing/Getty Images/National Geographic Creative; 131 (CTR RT), Ernie Janes/Nature Picture Library; (LO LE), Hellio & Van Ingen/NHPA/Photoshot; (UP LE), Kydpl Kyodo/AP Photo; 132 (LO), Shutterstock/Debbie Steinhausser; (CTR RT), Shutterstock/Chursina Viktoriia; (UP LE), Shutterstock/Horst Petzold; (CTR RT), Shutterstock/Alaettin Yildirim; 133 (CTR LE), Shutterstock/r.classen; (UP LE), Shutterstock/Eaglesky; (LO RT) Shutterstock/Ahturner; (UP RT), Shutterstock/E. O.; 134-135, Eric Beracassat/GAMMA/Getty Images; 136 (UP LE), Photo Researchers/FLPA; (LO), Daniel Heuclin/Nature Picture Library; 137 (LO CTR), FLPA/Fred Bavendam; (CTR RT), Alex Mustard/Nature Picture Library; (UP LE), Alex Mustard/Nature Picture Library; (CTR LE), Ingo Arndt/Nature Picture Library; 138 (LO), (Tony Gentile/Reuters/Corbis; (UP LE), Colouria Media/Alamy; (UP RT), Barry Cronin/Newsmakers/Getty Images; 139 (LO LE), Pilar Olivares/Reuters/Corbis; (LO RT), Dan Leeth/Alamy; (UP LE), Hemis/Alamy; 140-141, Shutterstock/pepmibastock; 142 (CTR LE), Imaginechina/Corbis; (UP LE), Panthera/Alamy; (LO LE), Yasuyoshi Chiba/AFP/Getty Images; 143 (UP LE), Imaginechina/Corbis; (LO LE), Yoshikazu Tsuno/AFP/GettyImages; (CTR RT), The Asahi Shimbun/Getty Images; 144-145, Sebastian Kaulitzki/Alamy; 145 (LO RT), Shutterstock/Sashkin; (UP RT), Shutterstock/Bo Valentino

CHAPTER 8

146-147, Jurgen Freund/Nature PL; 148 (UP LE), Richard Austin/Rex/REX USA; (LO LE), Richard Austin/Rex/REX USA; (CTR RT), Barry Bland/Rex/Rex/REX USA; 149 (LO), Press Association/Busch Gardens Tampa Bay/AP Photo;(UP LE), Richard Austin/Rex/REX USA; (CTR RT), Dimas Ardian/Getty Images; 150-151, Richard Bord/Getty Images; 152 (UP RT), Steve Speller/Alamy; (UP LE), Shutterstock/Tan Hung Meng; (LO), Peera Sathawirawong/123rf; 153 (UP LE), Ian Dagnall/Alamy; (CTR RT), WENN Ltd/Alamy; (LO), Shutterstock/dk tazunoki;154-155, Shutterstock/Aerostato; 156 (UP RT), Dave Watts/naturepl.com/NaturePL; (LO RT), Biosphoto/Brandon Cole/FLPA; (CTR LE), Loic Poidevin/Nature PL; 157 (LO LE), D. Parer & E. Parer-Cook/Minden Pictures/FLPA; (UP RT), John Downer Productions/NaturePL; (CTR RT), David Fleetham/NaturePL; 158-159, Trevor Payne/Alamy; 159, Shutterstock/johnfoto18; 160, DCarto/Dreamstime; 162 (UP LE), iStock/GlobalIP; (LO LE), iStock/GlobalIP; (CTR) iStock/milosluz (picture frame); (CTR LE), Marvin Dott/Westend61/Corbis; (LO RT), Twovogelart/Dreamstime; (CTR), Wikimedia Commons; 163 (LO LE), John Greim/LightRocket/Getty Images; (UP RT), Mannie Garcia/Reuters/Corbis; (LO RT), iStock/Antgain; (UP LE), Library of Congress; 164-165, Courtesy of Mosaïcultures Internationales de Montréal/Photo courtesy Espace pour la vie/Jardin botanique de Montréal (Claude Lafond);166 (UP RT), Les Stocker/Alamy; (UP LE), William West/AFP/Getty Images; (LO), World Illustrated/Photoshot; 167 (UP LE), Reuters/Corbis; (UP RT), Martin Harvey/NHPA/Photoshot; (CTR LE), Jurgen Freund/Nature PL; (LO), Suzi Eszterhas/Minden Pictures/FLPA

CHAPTER 9

168-169, Pete Oxford/NaturePL; 170, Shutterstock/Max Earey; 172 (LO), Joe Maher/WENN/Newscom; (UP LE), Caters News Agency; (UP RT), lachris77/123rf; 173 (UP RT), Tsheko Kabasia/Sowetan/Gallo Images/Getty Images; (CTR LE), Caters News Agency; (LO RT), Maor Zabar Hats/www.maorzabarhats.etsy.com; 174 (UP LE), Jan Woitas/dpa/Corbis; (LO LE), Norbert Wu/Minden Pictures/FLPA; (UP RT), Shutterstock/Christian Musat; (LO RT), Franco Banfi/NaturePL; 175 (LO LE), Anup Shah/NaturePL; (LO RT), Ronald Messemaker/Minden Pictures/FLPA; (UP LE), Shutterstock/Yongyut Kumsri; (UP RT), Shutterstock/Yongyut Kumsri; 176-177, Shutterstock/Africa Studio; 178-179, Shutterstock/Sekar B; 179 (CTR RT), Shutterstock/aastock; (UP LE), Shutterstock/Barnaby Chambers; (LO LE), Shutterstock/eastern light photography; 180 (LO RT), Pete Oxford/NaturePL; (CTR LE), Gerard Lacz/FLPA; 181 (LO LE), Birgitte Wilms/Minden Pictures/FLPA; (UP LE), Visuals Unlimited, Inc./David Wrobel/Getty Images; (LO RT), Decha Thapanya/123rf ; (CTR RT), MichelleSC/Shutterstock; 182-183, John Lopez Studio; 184-185, Rolf Nussbaumer Photography/Alamy

BACK MATTER

186 (UP RT), Shutterstock/Bork; 187 (LO RT), Jose Luis Pelaez/Getty Images; 188 (UP RT), Justin Lewis/Getty Images; 189 (LO RT), Chris Mattison/Alamy; 190 (UP RT), Mitsuhiko Imamori/Minden Pictures/FLPA

DID YOU JUST yawn?

Betcha did. Wonder why? If you've got a question, we've got answers! 1,111 of them, in fact, about all kinds of topics, from super silly to sorta serious, plus cool top 10 lists, activities, and more. Why do we yawn? Dream? Sneeze? Why do we get zits? Why don't we all speak the same language?

STAY CURIOUS!

WHY?
1,111 ANSWERS TO EVERYTHING
CRISPIN BOYER

AVAILABLE WHEREVER BOOKS ARE SOLD
Discover more at **kids.nationalgeographic.com**

NATIONAL GEOGRAPHIC KiDS

© 2015 National Geographic Society

For more information, please visit nationalgeographic.com, call 1-800-NGS LINE (647-5463), or write to the following address:
National Geographic Society
1145 17th Street N.W.
Washington, D.C. 20036-4688, U.S.A.

Visit us online at nationalgeographic.com/books

For librarians and teachers: ngchildrensbooks.org

More for kids from National Geographic: kids.nationalgeographic.com

For information about special discounts for bulk purchases, please contact National Geographic Books Special Sales: ngspecsales@ngs.org

For rights or permissions inquiries, please contact National Geographic Books Subsidiary Rights: ngbookrights@ngs.org

Hardcover ISBN: 978-1-4263-2068-2
Reinforced library binding ISBN: 978-1-4263-2069-9

Printed in the United States of America
15/RRDW-CML/1

ANATOMY OF A WEIRD BUT TRUE FACT

How does a fact make it into a Weird But True book?

First, it has to be **WEIRD.** Our team of editors and writers scour the news, the latest discoveries, Internet gems, crazy conversations, urban legends, wacky myths, and tantalizing tidbits to find a fact that's really weird.

It also has to be **TRUE.** So our team of researchers checks every single word to make sure the fact is 100 percent accurate.

It has to **LOOK COOL.** Our photo editors and designers find the perfect weird picture or the most dazzling weird design to make each fact jump out at you.

It has to **BE FUN.** Then we put it all together in a sensory overload presentation to knock your socks off.

Here's a weird-but-true fact about *Ultimate Weird But True 2:* It took an ultimate team of 4 editors, 1 writer, 3 designers, 4 photo editors, 2 researchers, plus lots of experts to make the weirdest, truest, most ultimate book around.